RYA SAIL TRIM
HANDBOOK
FOR CRUISERS

By Rob Gibson

ILLUSTRATIONS BY ANDREW SIMPSON

Best wishes Emma

Rob

© Rob Gibson 2010
First Published 2010 Reprinted 2011, 2012
Reprinted July 2013, June 2014, February 2015,
May 2016, August 2017, August 2018

The Royal Yachting Association
RYA House, Ensign Way, Hamble,
Southampton SO31 4YA
Tel: 02380 604100
Web: www.rya.org.uk
Follow us on Twitter @RYAPublications or on YouTube

We welcome feedback on our
publications at publications@rya.org.uk

You can check content updates for RYA publications at
www.rya.org.uk/go/bookschangelog

ISBN: 978-1906435-578

Cover Design: Velveo Design
Typeset: Velveo Design
Proofreading and indexing: Alan Thatcher
Printed: in China through World Print
Photographers: Paul Wyeth and Andrew Simpson

Sustainable
Forests

EMAS
VERIFIED
ENVIRONMENTAL
MANAGEMENT

FOREWORD

As a sailmaker all my working life and the founder in 1985 of Kemp Sails, sail trim is for me as natural as walking or riding a bike, but for many it can appear to be some kind of black art! When Rob asked me to write the foreword to his new book I was both honoured and excited at the prospect of introducing sail trim to new eyes.

Good sail trim is not just for high performance racers, any sailor will benefit from correctly set sails. Not only will the boat be more comfortable and safer, it will also sail faster as well. This may win you a regatta or a once a season race but it can just as easily get you into port before the tide changes. Imagine, there you are, sitting enjoying a well earned meal while your cruising companions are still out there slogging away, I know where I would like to be!

Correct sail trim is not just about performance or winning races, sails are a complicated product that can take many hours to build, the materials range from a fairly robust Polyester to ultra light weight membranes incorporating the very latest composite fibres so whether you have just purchased a simple roller genoa, or the newest membrane mainsail, you need to protect your investment. I am all too aware of how much sails cost, but as a sailmaker I would like to see you look after them and use them properly.

All the information you need to know is here – I hope it inspires as much fascination in sail trim with you as with me when I was a small child sailing his Mirror dinghy. Just remember sail trim is like riding a bike, the more you do it the better you get and if you fall off, climb back on and try again.

Rob Kemp
MD Kemp Sails

INTRODUCTION

If something's worth doing, it's worth doing it well! That's a good philosophy for life in general but particularly relevant to trimming sails. Good sail trim and the controls required to achieve it are not just for serious racers. Sails are the means of obtaining the best performance and, therefore, pride and pleasure from the considerable investment that we put into our boats.

It's often said that increasing your speed from five to five and a half knots will save you nearly an hour on a fifty mile passage, thereby offering a better choice of berth when you arrive as well as uncrowded showers and the certainty of a table in your favourite restaurant. This is all true, but for me the most important reason for improving sail trim is to provide comfort rather than boat speed. With the sails correctly trimmed most sailboats will more or less steer themselves, the balance will be improved and the boat will ride more easily through the water. Overall, life on board becomes easier for both crew and gear.

Having said that, I see nothing wrong with an extra hour in the yacht club nor the hour less spent dodging freighters in mid-passage. Fortunately, with the right knowledge and a few simple adjustments to the sails we can enjoy all of these benefits.

Rob Gibson

CONTENTS

FOREWORD 2

INTRODUCTION 3

1 HOW SAILS WORK **6**

Flow theory 7
Some fundamentals 9
Beating 12
Beam reach 12
Balance 13
Weather helm 14
Lee helm 14
Apparent wind / true wind 15

2 RIG TYPES **16**

Setting up the rig 17
Centring the mast 18
Adjusting the shrouds 19
Pre-bend 20
Checking the rig under sail 20

3 JIBS & GENOAS **21**

Foresails 21
Foresail controls 22
Roller reefing foresails 27

4 MAINSAILS **28**

Mainsail controls 28
Trimming the mainsail 33
Fully battened mainsails 34
Lazy jacks 35
In-mast reefing mainsails 36

5 REEFING **37**

Reefing a conventional mainsail ... 38

6 SAILING UPWIND **40**

Acting as one 40
Sails – small but perfectly formed ... 40
Light airs (Force 1 to 2) 41
Medium wind (Force 3 to 4) 41
Heavy winds (Force 5 and above) ... 42
Target speeds 42
Up-wind VMG 43
Lee bowing the tide 44
Wind shifts and squalls 44

7 REACHING **45**

Tracks and barber haulers 45
Reaching blocks 46
Whisker poles 46
Reaching sails 47
Hull speeds 47

8 DOWNWIND SAILING **48**

Preventers 48
Poling out headsails 49
Roll control 49
Mainsail or no mainsail? 50
Training runs – tacking downwind ... 50
Downwind VMG 51
Using waves 51
Gusts 51

9 TRADE WIND SAILING   **52**

Twin Headsails   53

10 SPINNAKERS   **54**

Asymmetric spinnakers   55
Setting a gennaker   55
Hoisting   56
Trimming   56
Reaching   56
Running   56
Gybing   57
Dropping   57
Rollers   57
Bowsprits   58
Snuffers   58
Packing spinnakers   58

11 SYMMETRICAL SPINNAKERS   **59**

Setting up   60
Hoisting   61
Trimming   62
Gybing – dip pole method   63
Gybing – end to end method   63
Dropping – by the head   64
Dropping – tripping the windward clew   65
Broaching   65

12 SAILS AND SAILCLOTHS   **66**

Laminates   67
Woven sailcloths   68
UV Protection   68
Spinnakers and gennakers   69

13 HEAVY WEATHER SAILS   **70**

Heavy weather jib   70
Trysail   71
Storm jib   71
Waves and heavy weather   72
Storm sailing   73
Heaving to   74

GLOSSARY   **75**

Sailmakers' terms   75

INDEX   **80**

MEMBERSHIP PAGES   **83**

CHAPTER 1

HOW SAILS WORK

Before discussing the mechanics of sail trim it's important that we review the terminology used to name the various parts of a sail, and also the way we define and describe sail shape.

Much of our sailing time is spent looking upwards at sails, a viewpoint that makes it easy to see their vertical shape. Yet, almost all descriptions refer to their shape in the horizontal plane – that's to say as the wind flows across the sail. Many sails have horizontal built in camber stripes allowing you to see their shape more clearly. But sometimes you have to lay on your back on the coach-roof or foredeck and look aloft to fully appreciate a sail's finer details.

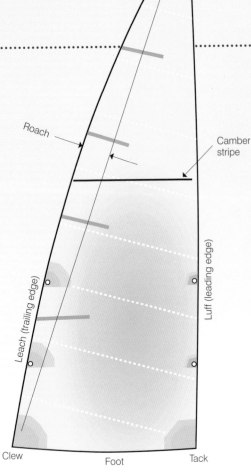

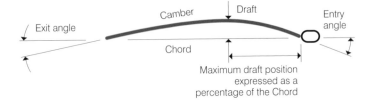

Flow theory

Sails harness the wind's energy by generating lift in much the same way an aeroplane's wings will lift it off the ground. There are similarities in their shapes and both sails and wings are known as aerofoils.

With sails the lift is generated by the flow of air across its surface horizontally from luff to leach. They are not flat sheets of fabric but are cut and fabricated so they form a shallow dish shape. To trim a sail we point the leading edge – the luff – directly into the wind and then pull the trailing corner – the clew – slightly across the wind. This sets up a steady airflow around both the concave (inside) surface and the convex (outside) surface of the sail.

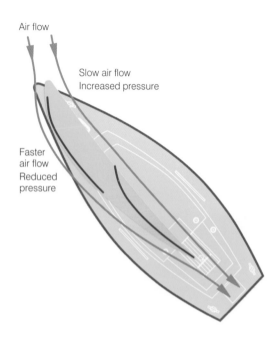

Air flow

Slow air flow
Increased pressure

Faster
air flow
Reduced
pressure

The Swiss physicist Daniel Bernoulli (1700–1782) discovered that a fluid's pressure reduces when it accelerates and increases when it slows down. Air follows this principle when flowing over a sail. The air flowing around the inside slows and its pressure builds. However air flowing around the outside of a sail flows more freely and speeds up, reducing the pressure. Since there is now a pressure difference on each side of the sail, it is drawn towards the faster flow on the outside, creating the lift that powers a boat.

You can test Bernoulli's Theorem by dangling the back of a spoon against the flow of water from a tap. The spoon will be pulled into the flow.

One might conclude that the deeper the dish shape – the more that the sail is curved – the bigger the pressure difference and the greater the power produced. But power isn't everything.

Look at *fig 4a*. It shows a boat flying a single mainsail having a nice even curved shape. The coloured arrows represent the forces produced by the pressure difference between the inside and outside of the sail. Because the sail has an even curve the forces are evenly spread. The green arrows are producing some drive and would like to pull the boat forward, but they are opposed by the yellow arrows wanting to drag it backwards. Their combined force will certainly heel the boat over but, otherwise, it isn't going anywhere. However the boat's entry angle to the wind is pretty good.

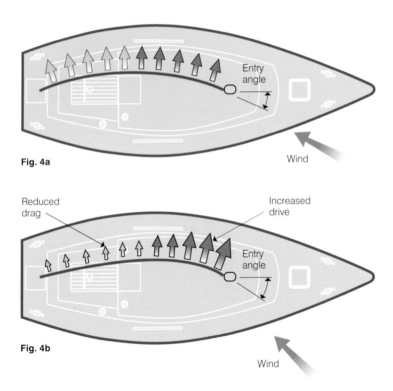

Fig. 4a

Fig. 4b

In *fig 4b* the same boat has a sail cut with more curve forward near the mast, and a flatter trailing section. Now you can see that there's more drive in the leading part of the sail, with the relatively flat trailing section experiencing much less pressure difference and, therefore, producing less drag. This boat stands a good chance of moving forward but the large entry angle means that it will not sail as close to the wind.

So, sails must first be cut by the sailmaker so they can take up the right shape, then trimmed by the crew so they work optimally. This will involve trying to shape the sails to match the entry angle to the wind direction while producing as much forward drive as possible.

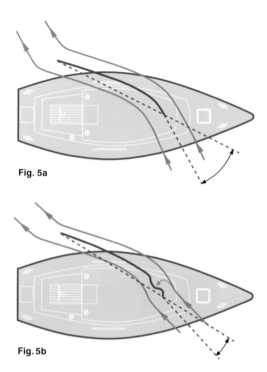

Fig. 5a

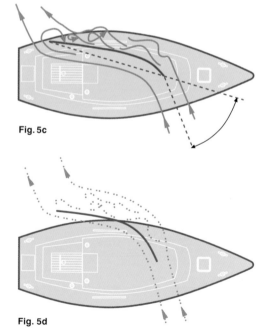

Fig. 5b

Fig. 5c

Fig. 5d

Some fundamentals

The entry angle is the angle between the chord of the sail, in plan view, and the wind direction. In *fig 5a* the sail's entry angle is good, with the leading edge pointing directly into the wind. The exit angle is also good. The airflow on both sides of the sail is smooth and attached to the sail's surface. This sail will provide good drive.

In *fig 5b* the entry angle is too small, the leading edge of the sail is flapping (luffing) in the disturbed airflow, and the sail is stalled (not working). It needs to be sheeted in, increasing the entry angle enough to stop the luffing.

Fig 5c shows a sail that's over sheeted. The entry angle is too large; the flow of air around the outside of the sail has become detached and turbulent. Air from the inside of the sail is being drawn around the leach to fill the void and the sail is stalled. It might look OK but without an accelerated, attached flow around the outside surface, the sail isn't providing any drive. The sheet should be eased so that the outside flow can reattach.

Fig 5d shows a full sail in a very light breeze. The airflow around the outside of the sail is simply too weak to remain attached to the surface, has broken away, and become disturbed. The sail should be flattened and the sheet eased so that the flow can re-attach to the outside surface.

TOP TIP

"Don't ask a small wind to do too much,"
is a very wise saying.

To maximise the effectiveness of sails, sheets must be adjusted to get the entry and the exit angles correct. Mostly, you will be sailing with two sails – a jib or genoa (foresail) and a mainsail. Those two sails will combine, effectively to produce one aerofoil so you need to consider the entry angle at the leading edge of the combined surface (the jib luff) and the exit angle at the trailing edge (the mainsail leach).

The best way to see the airflow across the sails and whether the entry and exit angles are correct is to use a series of telltales. These low tech. and low cost bits of kit, essentially small sticky pads and a short length of wool, will stream out straight and nearly horizontal in a smooth airflow, or lift and shake in a disturbed, turbulent flow, indicating immediately whether things are right or wrong.

Telltales should be placed on the inside and outside surfaces of a headsail 20cm (8 inches) or so from the luff. On the mainsail stick them on the leach close to the batten ends.

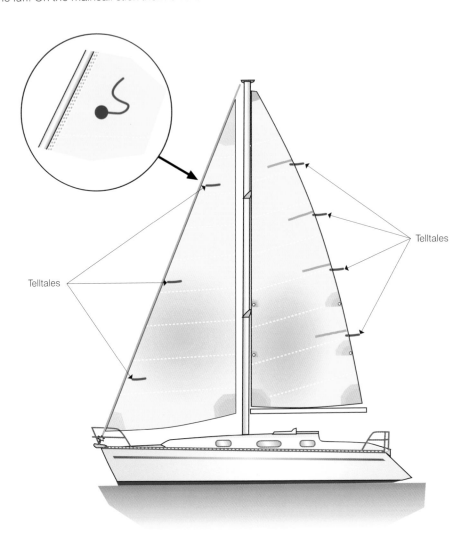

Telltales

Telltales

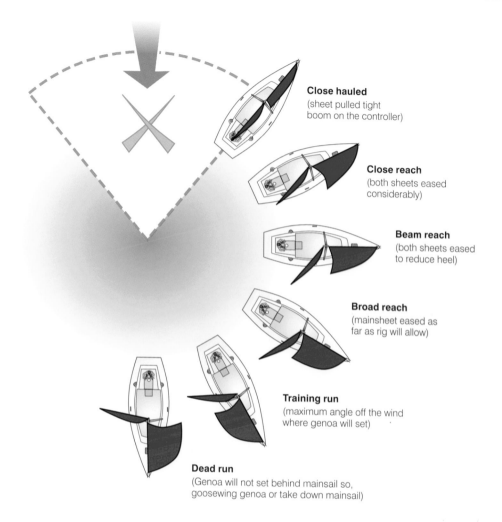

Close hauled
(sheet pulled tight
boom on the controller)

Close reach
(both sheets eased
considerably)

Beam reach
(both sheets eased
to reduce heel)

Broad reach
(mainsheet eased as
far as rig will allow)

Training run
(maximum angle off the wind
where genoa will set)

Dead run
(Genoa will not set behind mainsail so,
goosewing genoa or take down mainsail)

Let's look at sail settings for the various points of sail. If you look at the above illustrations you can see that the sails are being maintained at the same angles relative to the wind while the boat is rotated beneath them. Note how far the mainsail boom moved when the boat bore away from close hauled to the close reach, and how little movement is left when bearing away all the way to a broad reach.

It's very common to see sails that are over sheeted with helmsmen struggling to keep the boat on a straight course.

TOP TIP

As a general rule, ease the sheet until the sail just starts to luff (shake on the leading edge) then pull it in slowly, just enough to stop the luffing. Start from the front of the boat, in clear air, and work your way back. So jib first then mainsail!

Beating

In more detail, let's take a look at the driving forces, and the drag, when a sailboat is close hauled or beating to windward.

- The two sails are pulled as close to the boat's centreline as their sheet leads will allow. Most of the foresail and the leading part of the mainsail are producing forward drive (green arrows).
- The trailing part of the foresail and the middle part of the mainsail are producing drive to the side that will only result in heeling (yellow arrows).
- The trailing part of the mainsail is actually producing a negative drag force (orange arrows).

The net result of the combined sail force as you can see from the direction of the arrows is a lot of sideways, and a little bit of forward drive.

That drive is resisted by the drag of the hull and keel being driven sideways and the overall result is a lot of heel with a small amount of forward movement. Even that movement includes a loss of direction to leeward, known as leeway.

All in all then, sailing close hauled with lots of heel may be exciting but it's not very efficient.

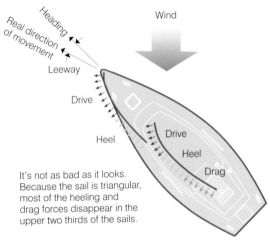

It's not as bad as it looks. Because the sail is triangular, most of the heeling and drag forces disappear in the upper two thirds of the sails.

Beam reach

Now compare the last situation with a beam reach.

The very full shape of the leading part (and majority of the area) of the foresail is producing lots of forward drive. The trailing edge, because the sail has to be sheeted back onto the boat, will produce a tiny bit of heel and even a tiny bit of drag, but the sail area involved is very small.

The mainsail is producing loads of forward drive and the net effect is lots of drive in the direction that the hull and keel were designed to follow, forward. Hull and keel drag are, therefore, minimised and the boat will speed forward on the most efficient point of sail.

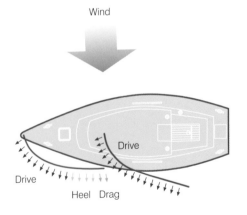

With almost no heeling and drag forces a yacht should sail almost upright on a beam reach.

Balance

Sailing efficiently involves balancing all of the forces at work on the boat to produce the maximum forward drive from the available wind. Take a look at the plan part of *fig 9*, and the forces at work on the boat. On the leeward side you can see the positive, aerodynamic forces split into the two components; the heeling force and the drive force, together with their resultant the total aero-force.

On the windward side are the negative forces; drag and hydro-lift with their resultant the total hydro-force.

When the driving aero-force exceeds the resisting hydro-force then the boat will move forward, but not in the direction indicated by the heading. There will be a loss to leeward and the direction of movement will be that shown by the solid line.

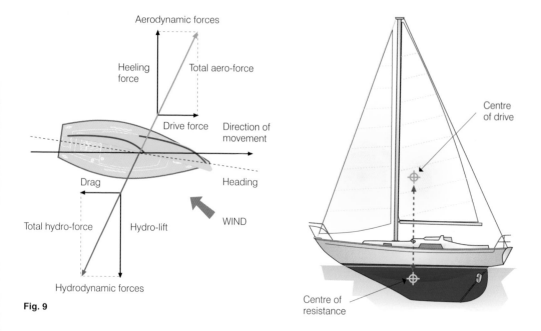

Fig. 9

The difference between the boat's heading and the course that it follows is known as leeway and some leeway is inevitable when a sailboat drives upwind. As a result of leeway, the boat's keel and rudder (when it's centred) have an entry-angle compared with the flow of water, and generate positive lift, helping to pull the boat forward and to windward.

The elevation part of *fig 9* shows the centre of drive over – but in line with – the centre of resistance so, while the boat will heel, it has no tendency to turn, either towards, or away from the wind. So the rudder can be centred, the boat will be light on the helm and easy to sail. In fact all sail boats should be easy to steer; to the extent that most can sail themselves in a straight line as long as the centre of drive is over and aligned with the centre of resistance and we achieve that balance by trimming the sails correctly.

Weather helm

Now let's upset the balance by taking down the foresail *(fig.10)*. The centre of drive will move aft relative to the centre of resistance, introducing a turning moment that will try to turn the boat into the wind. This effect is called weather helm. To counter it, the helm will have to be turned to leeward, whereupon the rudder lift will break down and become drag, slowing the boat.

Clearly, it's very important to maintain a proper balance between the hydrodynamic and aerodynamic forces. Keeping the centre of drive over the centre of resistance means less work for the helm, either human or autopilot, and the boat will move more easily through the water.

But it's an ongoing matter. A gust of wind, hitting the boat, will often power up the mainsail more than a jib, moving the centre of drive aft and inducing weather helm (the tendency to turn into the wind).

So, what should you do?

• When the wind increases, ease the mainsail sheet. Even if the luff bulges the heeling forces will be reduced, the forward drive forces maximised and the centre of effort moved forward again, restoring the balance in the boat.

You can change the size of the sails, both fore and aft of the mast, to alter the position of the centre of drive. We'll deal later with the mechanics of reefing – reducing the size of a sail whilst sailing – but suffice to say it should be carried out progressively to both foresail and mainsail in order to maintain good balance.

A bit of weather helm is helpful for two reasons: firstly, the boat will turn to the wind and lose drive if the helm is left unattended and, secondly, because a little extra lift and windward drive is created by a rudder turned slightly in the flow of water. Weather helm should be about 5° maximum.

Centre of drive

Centre of lateral resistance

Turning moment

Fig. 10

Lee helm

The opposite of weather helm is lee helm *(fig.11)*. This arises when the centre of drive moves forward, causing the boat to turn away from the wind. Lee helm is regarded as an entirely negative feature because an unattended sailboat will bear away and power up – perhaps even gybing. The rudder's lift will be negative, adding to the leeway.

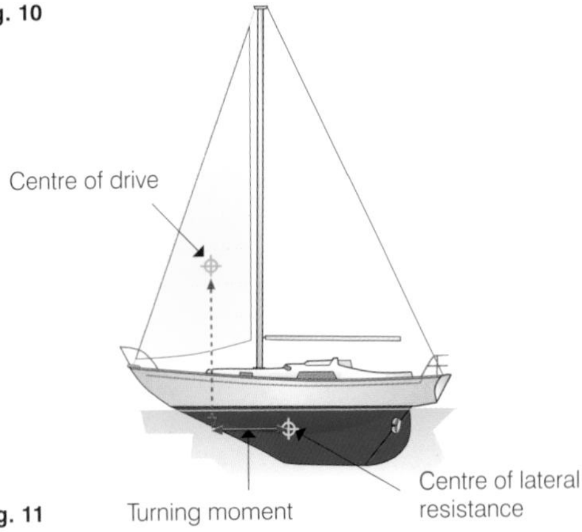

Centre of drive

Fig. 11   Turning moment

Centre of lateral resistance

Apparent wind / true wind

The issue of wind direction and strength becomes complicated as soon as a boat starts to move. Telltales and wind vanes on mastheads only indicate the true wind when a boat is stationary. As soon as it starts to move they react to a combination of wind and the boat's movement – apparent wind.

Fig 12a shows a vector diagram for a boat on a beam reach. The long side of the trapezoid represents 10 knots of true wind drawn to scale while the short side of the trapezoid shows the boat speed, 6 knots. The long diagonal represents the apparent wind. Note that the length of the line now shows 12 knots of wind speed and the angle of the wind crossing the boat has decreased to 60°. In order to maintain the same entry angle to the wind, the boat's mainsail and jib had to be trimmed on – meaning, pulled in – progressively as the boat accelerated.

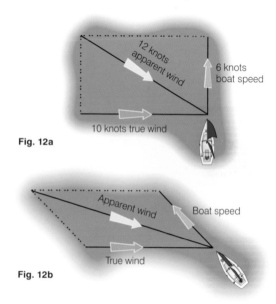

Fig. 12a

Fig 12b shows the apparent wind for the same conditions with the boat sailing close-hauled, at 45° to the true wind. You can see that the apparent wind builds significantly and the entry angle closes down as the boat accelerates forward to a full speed of 6 knots.

Fig. 12b

Fig 12c shows the same boat broad reaching at six knots in the same wind. This time the apparent wind decreases but the entry angle still closes down.

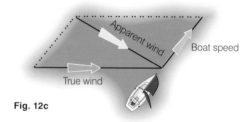

Fig. 12c

In all three of the illustrations the sails had to be considerably re-trimmed as the boat increased speed, and boat speed varies all of the time. Wind speed and direction are rarely constant, so it follows that, to keep a boat moving efficiently through the water, the sails need almost constant re-trimming to cope with the constantly changing conditions.

TOP TIP

Remember, as soon as you start moving the windex or woolies will only show you the apparent wind. The same is true of the more basic electronic wind insruments. To display true wind information the wind instrument must interface with the log, or speed input.

CHAPTER 2

RIG TYPES

Although not concerned here with the differences between sloops, ketches or schooners, or even between Bermudan and gaff rigs, I do need to describe the way that individual masts are designed and set up. Once you understand the general principles behind the setting of an individual mast, you can apply those principles to single and two-masted vessels and, to a lesser extent, even to gaff rigged boats.

Masthead sloop (Masthead rigs often feature deck stepped masts)

Most modern sailing cruisers are sloops (single masts) with either a masthead or a fractional rig. A masthead rig features a forestay that reaches to the top of the mast whereas a fractional rigged forestay will only reach part way to the top. A few years ago 3/4 fractional rigs (where the forestay reaches a point 3/4 of the way up the mast) were common.

Fig. 13

The modern trend, however, is for 7/8 or even 9/10 fractional rigs. Fractional rigged masts allow more control over mast bend while sailing but at the expense of some foresail area. Dedicated cruisers might find the tweakability of the fractional rig unnecessary and prefer the larger foresail and smaller mainsail option of the masthead rig.

3/4 fractional rig

7/8 fractional rig

Setting up the rig

I'm not suggesting that every sailor should be capable of adjusting their standing rigging – far from it. In fact, unless you are absolutely confident I suggest you employ a professional rigger to do it for you. Sailors should, however, be able to take a look at their rig, and decide when and if it's in need of adjustment, because a badly adjusted rig is unsafe. Here are the points to look out for and the adjustments that you should be aware of.

Rake: Mast rake is the angle (nearly always aft) off the vertical a mast is when viewed from the side. The yacht or rig designer will have chosen whatever rake they felt was best to balance the relationship between the keel and mast positions. But this still leaves scope for some fine tuning.

Adjusting the rake moves the centre of effort of the mainsail either backwards or forwards, either increasing or decreasing weather helm. So it's important that the rake is correct.

Very often the designed rake – usually expressed in degrees – will be recorded somewhere in the boat's papers or available from the manufacturer. Sometimes it can be measured from published drawings. Or you may have to measure the rake by dangling a weight from the main halyard on a calm day, then measuring the distance between the halyard and the back of the mast at the gooseneck *(fig 15)*.

It's worth noting that:

- With 1° of rake the mast will lean back 175mm (7 inches) for every 10 metres (33 feet) of mast height.

- With 2° of rake the mast will lean back 350mm (14 inches) for every 10 metres of mast height.

If you can't find any reliable information for your boat then 2° of rake is a good figure to start with. But you can also experiment and play by trial and error. When sailing with a full mainsail, close hauled, in about a Force 3 wind you should feel a couple of degrees of weather helm. If there's no weather helm increase the rake and if there's too much weather helm, decrease it.

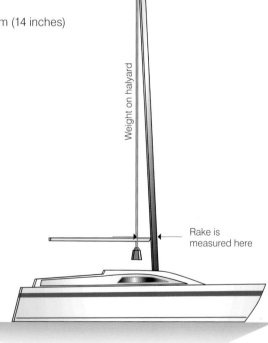

Weight on halyard

Rake is measured here

Fig. 15

Centring the mast

It should be unnecessary to say that the top of the mast must be over the centreline of the boat, but you'd be amazed at the number of rigs that are not properly centred. To check, pull the main halyard down tight to the chain plate on one side of the boat and then the other. With the same tension applied, the halyard should reach the same point on both sides. If not then ease off the short cap shroud and pull in the long one until the halyard shows the same measurement on both sides.

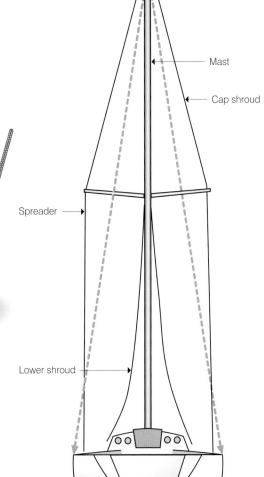

Mast

Cap shroud

Spreader

Lower shroud

Once you are sure that the mast is centred then any subsequent shroud adjustments must be made equally on both sides of the rig.

Now, while you are looking up, check the spreaders. The spreaders should bisect the angle made in the cap shroud as it passes over the spreader end. Droopy spreaders are unable to take the required compression load from the shroud and could lead to rig failure.

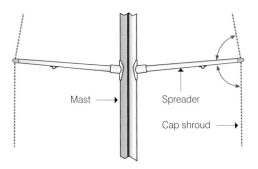

Mast → Spreader

Cap shroud →

TOP TIP

If you feel that your boat performs better on one particular tack, it may be that the rig is not centred.

Adjusting the shrouds

How tight should the cap shrouds be? Well you can use a tension meter to give you a tension of around 25% of the wire's breaking strain or you can simply tighten them as far as you can with small hand tools (no long levers) remembering that a tight rig is safer than a sloppy one.

With the mast centred and the shrouds tight we next need to make sure that the mast is straight. Masts work in compression and must remain in column when they are working. The wires used to keep them straight are the lower and intermediate shrouds. To check for straightness look up the mainsail track, you will see easily if the mast falls off one way or the other.

Fig 19 shows a two spreader rig that is definitely out of column. It falls off to the right, at the first spreader position, and to the left at the higher second spreader. To pull it back into a nice straight column it will be necessary to ease the right hand lower and the left hand intermediate while taking up the left hand lower and the right hand intermediate shrouds.

Lower and intermediate shrouds should not be as tight as the cap shrouds. If they are then loads can be transferred from spreader ends to the mast along the intermediate shroud allowing the upper part of the mast to bend to leeward under load, not a good thing! So give the lowers and intermediates just enough tension to keep the mast in column when loaded.

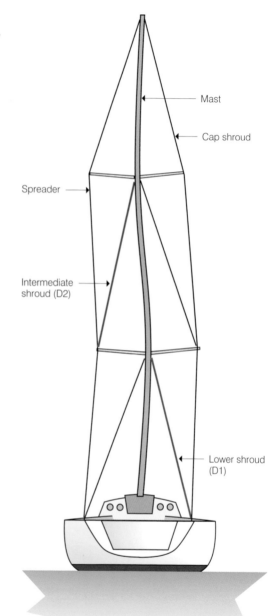

Mast

Cap shroud

Spreader

Intermediate shroud (D2)

Lower shroud (D1)

Fig. 19

Pre-bend

Most rigs are set up with a little bit of pre-bend. That is the bending of the mast into a bowed forward shape using the standing rigging. There are occasions when a mast can be subjected to considerable shock compression loads, for example, when a boat falls off a wave. In this circumstance a straight mast might bend forwards or backwards, but a mast with pre-bend will always bend more forwards. Bending forwards the mast will gain some support from the mainsail and is better able to resist buckling. A mast that bends backwards, or inverts as it's known will lose support and is very likely to buckle. It's worth pointing out here that you should be careful not to pull a mast into an inverted shape when sheeting hard on a deep-reefed mainsail or a tri-sail.

Pre-bend is measured by pulling the main halyard tight with the end held at the gooseneck. The pre-bend then is the maximum distance between the straight halyard and the bowed rear face of the mast. You can send somebody up the mast to measure that distance or express it as a percentage of the width of the mast at the same point – a judgement that can be made from deck level. A good sailmaker will measure your rig including the pre-bend before cutting the mainsail to suit, so make sure that you're consistent with the amount of pre-bend that you put into the mast.

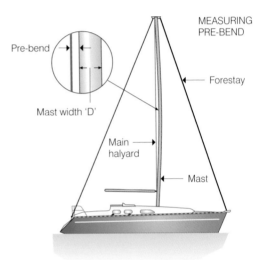

MEASURING
PRE-BEND

Pre-bend

Mast width 'D'

Forestay

Main
halyard

Mast

To set up the pre-bend with a masthead rig, simply pull the mast forward at spreader level using the inner forestay or forward facing lower shrouds. With a fractional rig with swept back spreaders pull down equally on the cap shrouds until the mast shows something over the required pre-bend then pull the mast back to the required setting using the lower shrouds.

TOP TIP

In the absence of any other information set up pre-bend of between 25% and 50% 'D', where 'D' is the width of the mast viewed from the side.

Checking the rig under sail

You can roughly set up a rig alongside but, to make the final adjustments, you need to go sailing. Pick an area with flat water and a day that allows you to sail with a full mainsail and a moderate heel when close hauled. Now sail close hauled and check for slackness in the leeward shrouds. If they are slack take out most of the slackness taking careful note of the number of turns that you make in the rigging screws, then tack and make the same adjustments on the other side. Repeat the exercise until the leeward shrouds remain tight and then check to make sure that the mast is still in column. A well-adjusted rig will give you a balanced sail and allow your sailmaker's best efforts to perform to their optimum.

CHAPTER 3

JIBS & GENOAS

Foresails

Foresails, also called headsails or forestaysails are sails that have their luff attached to the forestay. They are commonly known as genoas when they overlap the mainsail and jibs if they don't. Genoas will always be cut close to the deck, while jibs are often cut with a higher foot – Yankee style. Most skippers will refer to their collection of foresails by number, the No. 1 is the largest and the storm jib the smallest. Sailors also refer to foresails by the size of the sail relative to the fore triangle of the rig. The fore triangle is represented by the 'J' measurement, the distance between the root of the forestay and the leading edge of the mast, while the sail is represented by the LP measurement, the length of a line drawn perpendicular from the luff of the sail to the clew.

The table shows a typical selection of foresails for a modern sailing cruiser:

Sail No.	Cut	Size
No. 1	Genoa	150%
No. 2	Genoa	125%
No. 3	Genoa	100%
No. 4	Jib	75%
Storm	Jib	

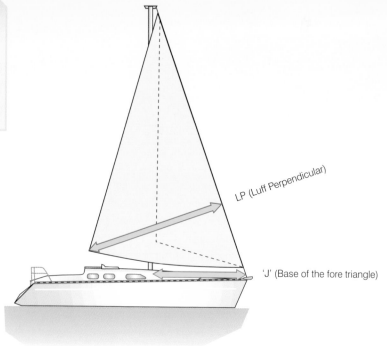

LP (Luff Perpendicular)

'J' (Base of the fore triangle)

Foresail controls

Many cruising sailors prefer to have one furling genoa rather than a selection of hanked sails. Whatever their size or cut sails can all be shaped to best advantage using the same four basic controls.

1 Backstay Not the most obvious control for foresails and therefore, often overlooked. Tension in the backstay controls tension in the forestay. A tight, straight forestay (therefore a straight foresail luff) will enable you to sail closer to the wind, it does this by reducing the entry angle and the heeling forces by flattening the sail and making it less powerful.

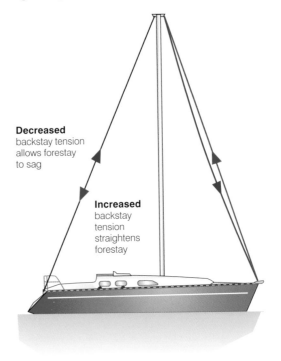

Decreased backstay tension allows forestay to sag

Increased backstay tension straightens forestay

Conversely, easing the backstay allows the forestay to sag making the foresail fuller and more powerful but increasing the entry angle.

From the foresail's point of view, backstay tension should be increased when sailing close hauled in moderate to strong winds but eased when sailing in very light breezes or reaching.

Many cruising yachts don't have instantly adjustable backstays, in which case they should be set up with plenty of tension, optimising the rig for strong upwind wind conditions when the rig loads are at a maximum.

2 Halyard tension Tightening and relaxing the halyard will move the sail's draft forward and backwards. Remember, the draft is the point of maximum depth in the sail, viewed in plan. When a foresail is first hoisted, this should be about 40% of the way back from the luff. Lay down on the foredeck and look up through the sail to judge the draft's position. Once you have the sail set up correctly, a good tip is to mark the halyard where it runs into the clutch or mark a stripe across the sail's luff tape and the luff groove on the forestay. Then it can be hoisted to exactly the right tension next time.

A typical backstay tensioner.

TOP TIP

Incidentally, if you notice a vertical crease appear next to the luff of the sail you already have too much halyard tension.

Increasing halyard tension moves the maximum draft forward to approximately 35% of the distance back from the luff. That concentrates drive at the leading edge of the sail, where it's most effective, and reduces the heeling and drag forces in the flattened trailing section. The entry angle of the sail will now not be as small as it was. This is a good set up for close-hauled sailing in stronger winds, or for reaching.

Slackening the halyard has the opposite effect, allowing the draft to move aft. At about 50% of the distance from the luff, the sail will take up the shape of an evenly balanced dish, forward drive will be reduced and the entry angle to the wind will decrease allowing you to sail slowly closer to the wind. A set up then to favour in very light winds when close-hauled and trying to make the best progress to windward.

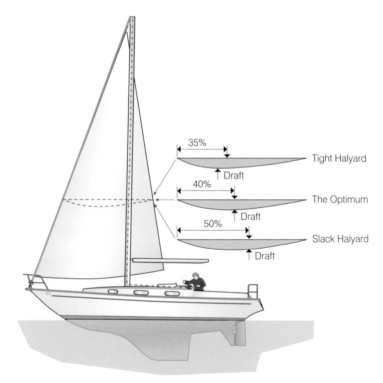

TOP TIP

If you find that you cannot pull the draft position forward to even the 50% position then it's time for a new sail!

TOP TIP

If you are using a furling genoa that will remain rolled on the forestay, remember to let the halyard tension off before you go home.

3 Sheet lead position Most sailing cruisers have moveable genoa cars running on lengths of track on each side deck. Some have to be moved by hand by pulling a plunger and dropping it into another locating hole. Others have lines and tackle attached often called towed cars enabling them to be moved from the cockpit under load.

Moving the car backwards and forwards changes the lead angle of the sheet to the sail and changes the relative tensions in the sail's leach and foot. This changes its shape considerably.

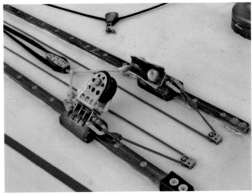

Adjustable towed genoa cars on inner and outer tracks.

In the illustrations we see the same foresail sheeted in hard for close hauled sailing but with three different car positions.

The car is too far forward. There's too much sag in the foot and the leach is pulled down tight and almost straight.

The car has been eased back a little and there is an even tension in the foot and the leach. The curvature of the foot is matched by the curve in the leach and the drive area will be well forward. This is a well set sail!

The car has moved back further. The foot has pulled tight and the leach has opened considerably allowing the top of the sail to twist forward. The sail will have flattened and is therefore de-powered.

4 Sheet tension It's the foresail sheets that will get the most attention as we work to keep the luff of the sail pointing into the wind. With every change of wind direction or course, the sheet tension needs to be re-set. Easing or trimming a mainsheet maintains a constant mainsail shape as the boom swings in and out. However, when easing a foresail sheet, the sail shape changes immediately. It becomes fuller, more powerful, and the draft moves forward, providing more forward drive as the sheet is eased. When the sheet is trimmed on the sail is flattened (less powerful) and the draft moves aft, producing more heel.

The foresail is trimmed on tight for close-hauled sailing. The sail *(fig 25a)* has an even shallow camber over its whole width producing an excellent entry angle, plenty of heel, and a little forward drive.

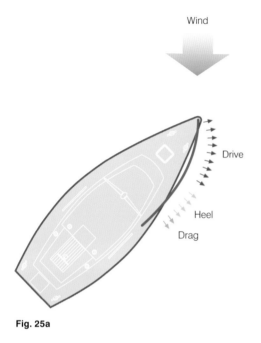

Wind

Drive

Heel

Drag

Fig. 25a

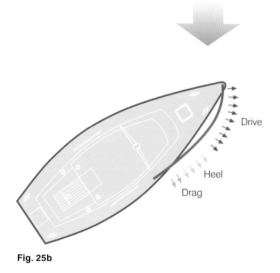

Wind

Drive

Heel

Drag

Fig. 25b

The sail *(fig 25b)* has been eased to allow the boat to bear away by 10% and keep a proper entry angle. The sail shape has changed considerably, the draft has moved way forward and will produce lots more forward drive while the flatter after section of the sail will produce less heel.

You can see that there are big gains to be made in forward drive if you can bear away just a little from close hauled.

Telltales These aren't really controls but are invaluable for demonstrating how the airflow is behaving around sails. On a foresail use three pairs, one near the top of the sail, one in the mid section and another about a metre above the tack. It's best if you use different colours in the pairs, red on the port face of the sail and green on the starboard face.

Remember for a well-trimmed sail you should expect to see a straight and positive flow around the outside of the sail and a slower flow around the inside. The flow should also be even from the bottom to the top of the sail.

There are simple rules for responding to the telltales:

- If the outside telltales lift you should ease the sheet out (or steer upwind a little).
- If the inside telltales lift you should trim the sheet in (or bear away).

In *fig 26a* the outside, green telltales are streaming nicely and the inside, red ones are just starting to lift. Perfect! And the flow is clearly constant all of the way up the sail.

Fig. 26a

In the next, *fig 26b*, the top inside telltale is lifting badly while the bottom one is fine so we don't want to trim on further or we will spoil the bottom of the sail. Taking the genoa car forward will reduce the twist in the sail and bring the top telltale into line without increasing the sheet tension.

Fig. 26b

In *Fig 26c* again the bottom and mid section telltales are OK, but the top outside one is lifting badly. This time the genoa car should be eased back until the top outside telltale streams nicely, leaving the shape of the bottom part of the sail unaltered.

For really effective foresail trimming you need to think beyond the sheet alone and start to use all four of the controls simultaneously.

Fig. 26c

Roller reefing foresails

Although something of a compromise, one cannot dispute the usefulness of roller reefing foresails. They are a great facility to get rid of the sail simply by pulling on a line from the cockpit. It's obvious that no sailmaker can produce sails that suit all conditions. A sail made heavy enough to survive strong winds when part reefed will be too heavy when fully deployed in light airs. Also, as soon as you take in more than a couple of rolls, the luff tends to lose tension and there's a lot of disturbance to the airflow around the now bulky leading edge. Nonetheless, I would certainly recommend their use for short-handed sailing.

Personally, I favour the idea of having two rolling genoas: One of 150% in a lightish material for days when the wind is unlikely to exceed Force 3, and another heavier, 110% sail to cope with a Force 4 to 5 wind and reef well for heavier breezes. Having a choice of sails allows you to take the sails off the forestay between cruises keeping them in good condition and extending their life.

Most sailmakers cut a rolling genoa flatter than a conventional sail so that it will roll away tidily. Some introduce foam pads behind the luff in the middle section to pad out the roll when the sail is reefed, reducing the fullness of the remaining sail area. Some also step the weight of cloth used in the sail's construction so that lighter material near the luff will roll away first as the sail is reefed.

Should you decide to use reefing foresails, don't skimp on the gear. If you fit equipment that's too light, it will let you down at just the wrong moment – perhaps when the breeze is rising and the foil starts to bend. You must also be prepared to adjust the genoa car position whenever you roll away or let out more sail (see *fig 27*).

When the genoa is rolled onto the forestay the genoa car must move forward if the correct sheet lead is to be maintained

Genoa car positions

Fig. 27

TOP TIP

If you're going to leave your foresail on the forestay between cruises, be sure it has a strip of UV protective material along the leach and foot to act as a cover when the sail is furled. Be sure to leave the boat with a tight roll in the sail and a couple of extra turns of sheet around it.

Many unattended rolling genoas have blown open in strong winds and flogged to destruction. Take a look at the halyard arrangement on a rolling foresail and make sure your crew are familiar with the method for dropping the sail. If your furling gear fails you may need to take down the foresail in a hurry!

CHAPTER 4

MAINSAILS

Mainsail controls

On most cruising boats the genoa is the primary source of forward drive not the mainsail. However the mainsail serves a very important purpose, balancing the turning effect of the foresail and rudder. So good mainsail trim is essential if you want an easy ride and steering. Because it's supported on two sides there are lots of ways of adjusting the mainsail's shape. Now let's take a look at the various controls, not all cruising yachts will have all of these controls, but if you understand their functions you will be able to make better use of those that you do have.

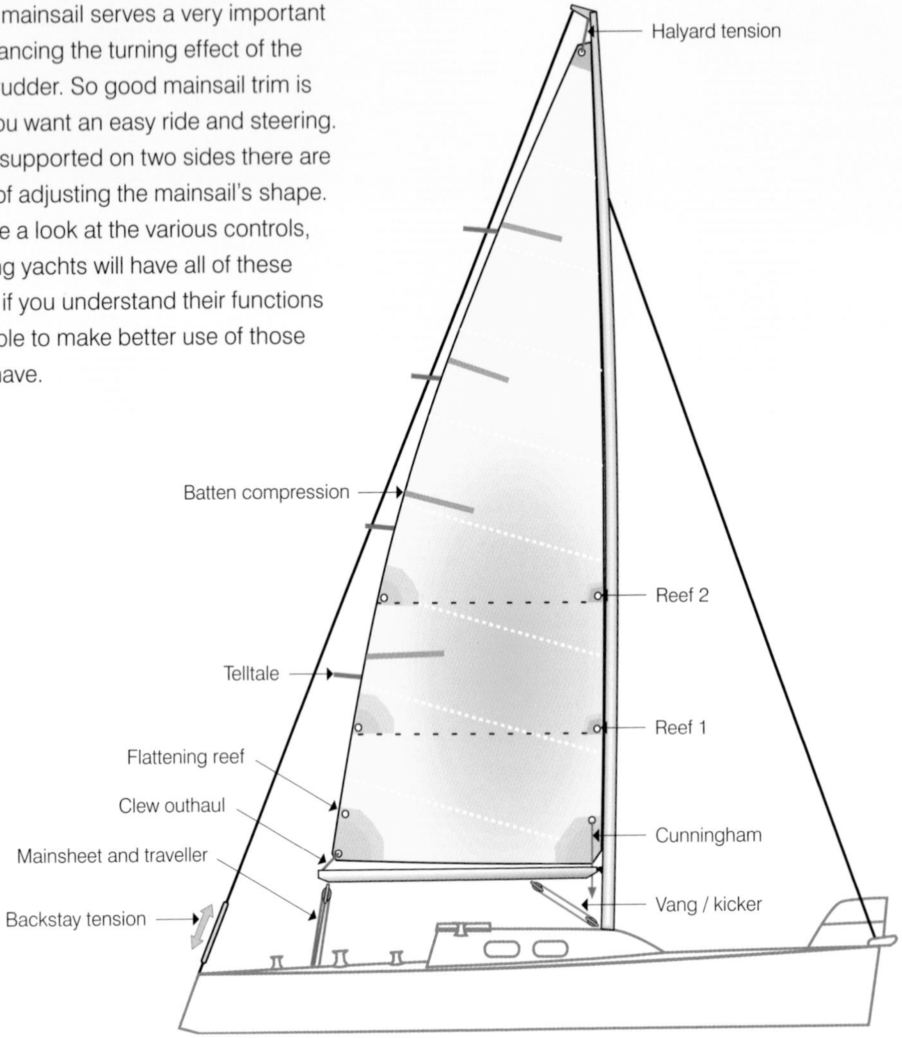

Halyard tension

Batten compression

Reef 2

Telltale

Reef 1

Flattening reef

Clew outhaul

Cunningham

Mainsheet and traveller

Backstay tension

Vang / kicker

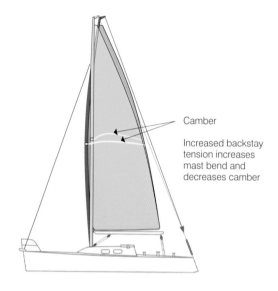

Camber

Increased backstay tension increases mast bend and decreases camber

Backstay: Increasing backstay tension will induce more forward bend in the mast. This will take some of the fullness out of the mainsail, flattening it. A flatter sail will have a smaller entry angle to the wind enabling you to sail higher. It will also be less powerful, reducing heel and weather helm.

Halyard tension / Cunningham: As with the foresail, increasing halyard tension will pull the draft forward and flatten the aft section of the sail. Flattening the majority of the sail will decrease heel and weather helm, while the more powerful forward section of the sail will give more forward drive when reaching. The entry angle to the wind is increased so in theory, you can't sail as close to the wind. However, when close hauled you will often tolerate a bit of luffing near the mast in order to gain the benefits of flattening the rest of the sail.

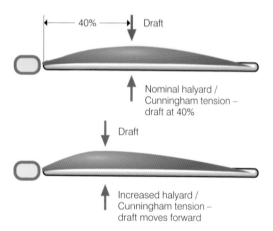

40% — Draft

Nominal halyard / Cunningham tension – draft at 40%

Draft

Increased halyard / Cunningham tension – draft moves forward

With all those sail slides, there's a lot of friction along a mainsail's luff so hauling on the halyard will often have no effect on the lower sections of the sail. Instead it's better to use a downhaul – often a block and tackle – attached just above the tack of the sail to pull down against the halyard to increase luff tension. This device is known as a Cunningham.

Cunningham is the name given to a downhaul tackle that increases luff tension in the lower part of a sail

Clew outhaul: The phrase is self-explanatory. The clew outhaul pulls the mainsail's clew out along the boom. This, too, will flatten the sail and move the draft aft and open (slacken) the leach a little. The entry angle to the wind decreases making it a good set-up for close-hauled sailing.

Easing the clew outhaul has the opposite effect. It will create a much fuller, and more powerful, sail with the draft further forward. It's also a good way of increasing the entry angle to the wind without letting the boom out, so ease the clew outhaul for reaching and running.

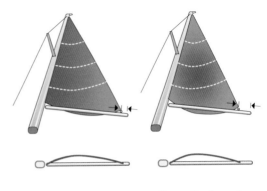

Clew outhaul tightened –
draft decreased,
sail flattened

Clew outhaul eased –
draft will increase and
move foreward

Kicking strap or vang: Also often known as a kicker, this is used to control the height of the boom and, therefore, the amount of twist in the sail – particularly when the boom is eased beyond the extent of the mainsheet traveller as it would be when running or reaching.

Easing the kicking strap will allow the boom to rise, opening the mainsail's leach, thereby increasing twist. Conversely, pulling on the kicking strap will close down the leach and decrease twist.

Good nominal set –
Top batten parallel
with boom

Too much twist –
Top batten falling
away to leeward

TOP TIP

Releasing the kicking strap altogether is a very good way of de-powering the mainsail quickly in an urgent situation such as a broach!

Kicker too tight –
Top batten points
to windward

Mainsheet: On most boats the mainsheet is the mainsail's primary control line and is used to adjust the sail's angle of attack with the wind. However, when sailing close hauled the sheet will be nearly vertical and can be used to adjust the leach tension. Easing the sheet will allow the leach to open while sheeting on will close down the leach.

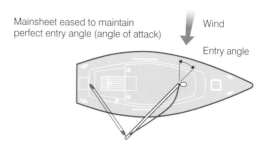

Mainsheet eased to maintain perfect entry angle (angle of attack)

Wind

Entry angle

Mainsheet traveller: Many mainsheets are anchored to a moving car running on a short length of athwartships track. The mainsheet traveller, as the arrangement is known, is only effective while the boom is over the track (sailing close hauled or close reaching) but, in those circumstances, it's a very useful tool used in conjunction with the sheet and kicking strap (vang).

For instance, when sailing close hauled and having worked hard to obtain the perfect mainsail shape, you need only ease the traveller down the track if you have to bear away a few degrees or want to de-power the mainsail in a gust. With the crisis over, you simply return the traveller to where it was and all is as before.

Heavy gusts

Traveller down to de-power mainsail

Traveller back up to return to sailing

When beating in light conditions it helps to haul the traveller up and ease the kicking strap and mainsheet to increase twist while keeping the boom on the centreline. In stronger breezes you can do the opposite – let the traveller down the track and haul in on the mainsheet to close down the leach.

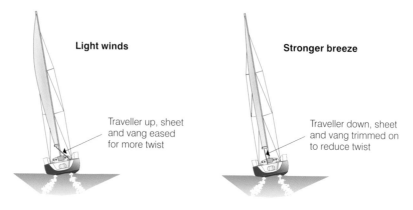

Light winds

Traveller up, sheet and vang eased for more twist

Stronger breeze

Traveller down, sheet and vang trimmed on to reduce twist

Flattening reef: Cruising mainsails often feature a cringle about 20 centimetres (8 inches) above the clew. If you pull that cringle down to the boom with a reefing pennant, the boom will lift and a lot of the fullness will disappear from the lower part of the sail. The resulting sail shape will give a much improved upwind performance.

The flattening reef is particularly useful on older, stretched sails, granting them another lease of life for working close hauled (see photo).

A flattening reef being applied on an old Dacron mainsail.

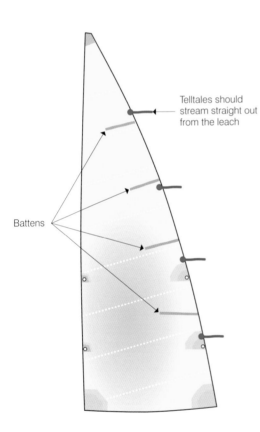

Telltales should stream straight out from the leach

Battens

Telltales... again: Remember that with mainsails we are most interested in the airflow off the leach of the mainsail (the exit angle) so this is where you should place them. We want to see them all flying straight out from the trailing edge of the sail. Play the sheet and traveller controls until the lower telltales stream nicely and then increase or decrease the sail's twist until the top ones behave similarly.

Don't ignore the top telltale. It can be difficult to make it fly but the mainsail isn't shaped properly until it does.

Batten compression: Battens are used to hold out the roach of the sail. They sit in sleeves sewn to the sail and can be compressed – more or less – by means of laces or Velcro tabs usually at the opening on the leach of the sail. Not enough compression and the batten won't provide enough support, while too much compression will induce an unwanted curve in the sail fabric.

TOP TIP

Many conventionally battened mainsails will have a full-length batten at the top of the sail. The compression in those full-length battens can be set very accurately using a set-screw near the batten car. Set the compression to give only a gentle camber to the top of the sail as you won't be able to flatten that part of the sail later using other controls.

Trimming the mainsail

When wind blows over the surface of the water friction occurs between the two fluids. As you go up the mast of a sailboat away from the water's surface the effect of friction reduces and the wind will attack the sail slightly differently. The wind shear as the effect is known allows you to twist the tops of your sails to take advantage of the increased entry angle of the high level wind.

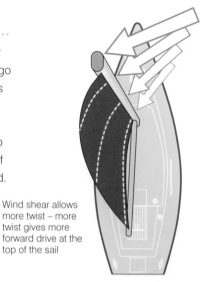

Wind

Wind shear increases from the bottom to the top of the mast

Wind shear allows more twist – more twist gives more forward drive at the top of the sail

Wind shear is a feature of light winds when the difference in direction is most pronounced

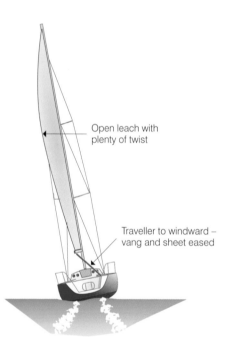

Open leach with plenty of twist

Traveller to windward – vang and sheet eased

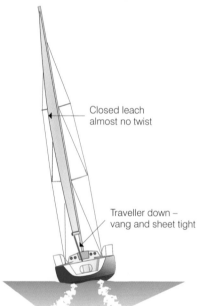

Closed leach almost no twist

Traveller down – vang and sheet tight

Sailing upwind, close-hauled in light airs: Keep the mast straight for a powerful sail shape. Have the clew outhaul a little less than tight and a relatively slack halyard and/or Cunningham. Keep the boom on the centreline with the traveller to windward and the sheet and kicker eased to give as much twist as the telltales will allow.

Close-hauled in heavy airs: Tension up the halyard and/or Cunningham, pull the clew outhaul tight and increase the backstay tension – all in the interest of flattening the sail. Drop the traveller car down just below the centreline of the boat and then increase sheet tension to close down the leach (decrease twist).

If the helm is at all heavy: Ease the traveller down to decrease weather helm and reduce the heel. Boat speed will increase and steering will be much easier. Always look for a good balance. Be prepared to accept some back-winding (luffing) of the mainsail near the mast in favour of an easy ride.

As you bear away onto a reach:

Straighten the mast and ease the clew outhaul to increase the power in the sail, take in any slack in the kicking strap and then ease the mainsheet to obtain the best entry angle to the wind.

Avoid easing the mainsheet to the extent that you close down the slot between the mainsail and the genoa. Think about easing the clew outhaul to improve the entry angle while holding the boom closer to the centreline.

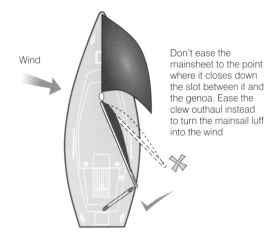

Wind

Don't ease the mainsheet to the point where it closes down the slot between it and the genoa. Ease the clew outhaul instead to turn the mainsail luff into the wind

Fully battened mainsails

The first fully battened sails were built for rigs with very high roach mainsails, not common on cruising monohulls. However, the use of full length battens on moderately roached sails has become popular with cruising skippers, despite their relatively high price.

The most obvious advantage is that once the battens are correctly set up obtaining a good sail shape is easy although some of the more subtle controls that we have discussed become ineffective with the rather rigid nature of the sail. They tend not to flog in the same way that a soft battened mainsail will which should be good for durability, but that can be a disadvantage, say, if you want to de-power the sail when manoeuvring slowly onto a mooring.

The car on this full length batten runs in the mast's luff groove. Some will run on a purpose made track mounted on the back of the mast.

Used on a boat with swept-back spreaders, fully battened mainsails can be awkward when the mainsheet is eased, since the battens can invert or take up an 's' shape when pressed against the shrouds. Also, each batten imposes a compression load on the mast, so the batten cars that carry them need to be quite sophisticated to run smoothly.

One of the most attractive features of fully battened sails is that, when used in conjunction with a lazy jack system, they flake neatly onto the boom making them exceptionally easy to stow.

Because catamarans don't have a backstay on the centre line they can carry mainsails with a very high roach. Full length battens are required to support that sort of sail shape.

Lazy jacks

Comprised of a web of light line rigged between the mast and boom on both sides of the mainsail. When deployed their purpose is to catch the sail when dropped, holding it up off the deck. There's no doubt that they make life much easier for short handed crews. Traditional lazy jacks can be pulled forward, clear of the sail, both reducing the possibility of wear and also keeping them out of the way when the sail is hoisted. It has become popular to integrate lazy jack lines with zip-up mainsail covers that are permanently rigged to the boom.

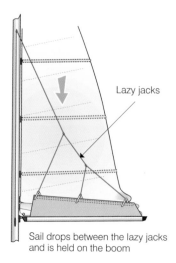

Lazy jacks

Sail drops between the lazy jacks and is held on the boom

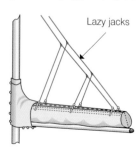

Stacking system featuring a permanently rigged zip-up sail cover

Lazy jacks

The sail is dropped between the lazy lines that hold the flaked sail on the boom. These lazy jacks are attached to the canvas sides of a permanently rigged sail cover or stacking system.

When the sail is stowed the cover can be zipped up and with the addition of a shroud around the gooseneck the mainsail is fully protected from the effects of weather and UV light.

In-mast reefing mainsails

Although very convenient, these systems impose limitations on the way such mainsails are cut, since the sail must be rolled up neatly inside the mast and be very flat and have no – or even negative – roach. Like the furling foresail, a furling mainsail is a compromise. If you choose an in-mast furling mainsail over a conventional sail then you will lose sail area and sail power plus many of the sail shaping controls. However, they are easy to reef, with an infinite range of settings and quick to stow.

To provide power in a furling mainsail you have to work very hard with the clew outhaul to provide just the right amount of camber for the point of sail, the entry angle and the wind strength. It's very easy to make the sail so flat that it becomes ineffective.

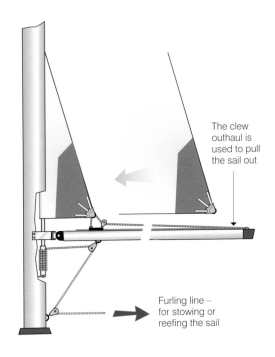

The clew outhaul is used to pull the sail out

Furling line – for stowing or reefing the sail

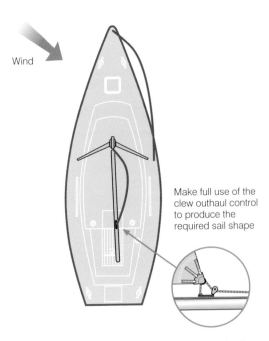

Wind

Make full use of the clew outhaul control to produce the required sail shape

Clew outhaul

On boats with swept-back spreaders the extra clew outhaul control can be a real advantage. When close reaching you can keep the boom relatively close to the centreline and ease the clew outhaul to create loads of camber while keeping the sail off the spreaders. The furling main will react very much like a genoa, in that as soon as the clew is eased, the draft will move well forward producing lots of forward drive while leaving a very flat after section.

The problem I personally have with the system comes from the potential for gear failure when the sail is part furled, or unfurled. Furling gear is not foolproof and the thought of having a part furled mainsail stuck up the mast with no way of stowing it in a high wind is frankly frightening!

CHAPTER 5

REEFING

Reefing is the process of reducing sail area in order to cope with stronger winds. Most helms will feel the need to reef as the steering becomes heavier with weather helm. If you're sailing close hauled, and have already eased the mainsail traveller but are still experiencing too much weather helm then it's time to start reefing.

Large overlapping genoas produce weather helm as well as mainsails so if you are sailing with a full 150% genoa then that's the place to start reefing. But if you only have a 100% jib set, then start by reefing the mainsail. It's important to try to match the sail areas both forward and behind the mast to keep the rig balanced. As an example a 10.6 metre (35 ft) cruiser with a conventional mainsail having three reef points will probably follow the following reefing sequence as the wind rises:

Wind force	Foresail size	Mainsail size
F 1 / 2	No.1 (150%) Genoa	Full Mainsail
F 3 / 4	No.2 (115%) Genoa	Full Mainsail
F 5	No.3 (95%) Jib	1st Reef in Mainsail
F 6	No.3 (95%) Jib	2nd Reef in Mainsail
F 7	No.4 (75%) Jib	Fully Reefed Mainsail

If you have a furling foresail or mainsail you can work entirely by feel progressively rolling away a sail to keep the weather helm within reasonable limits. Many furling sails have marks (usually spots) at intervals along the foot so that you have reference points to work to as you progressively roll away the sail area.

TOP TIP

Don't leave reefing too late, remember the old saying 'If you are thinking about reefing, do it! But if you are thinking about taking out the reefs, have a cup of tea first.'

Reefing a conventional mainsail

A typical conventional cruising mainsail will have three reef points – it can be made smaller (reefed) in three stages. When the third reef is put in only about 40% of the original luff length will be left up the mast so the remaining sail area is very small when compared with the full sail. As each reef is put in the unwanted part of the mainsail can be rolled up neatly and secured using light lines through small cringles (reinforced holes) in the body of the sail. If the mainsail is loose footed then those light lines should only pass around the sail, not the boom, in case the reefing pennant was to fail. If the lines must pass around the boom then a strong tie should be secured through the main reefing cringle and around the boom, again to guard against the failure of the reefing pennant.

The most common reefing system for mainsails involves a single reefing pennant at each reef point. In basic terms the mainsail is lowered just enough to hook the first reef cringle in the luff over the cowhorn, (a hook near the gooseneck). Once the halyard has been re-tensioned the first reefing pennant can be pulled tight, bringing the first reefing cringle in the leech down to the boom.

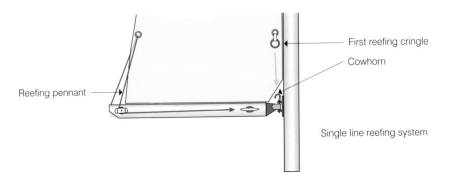

First reefing cringle

Cowhorn

Reefing pennant

Single line reefing system

The advantage of the two line system is that the whole operation can be accomplished from the cockpit, so nobody has to go leaping around on deck in rough seas or at night. Essentially the reef can be put in by pulling on two reef lines, first the luff line as the halyard is eased, and then, once the halyard has been re-tensioned and secured, the leach line. The disadvantage of the system is that you end up with an awful lot of lines leading back to individual clutches in the cockpit.

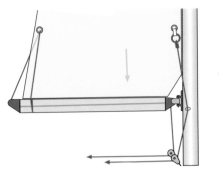

Two line reefing system

On the face of it the Jiffy system gives you the best of all options. One line at each reef point and no need to go up to the mast. It is a good system and can make life easy. The only problem comes from the friction that builds up with the many turns in the reefing pennant. The pennant is heavy to pull in and the line therefore is put under considerable loads and, when you want to shake out the reef the pennant is again difficult to pull back through the system.

Jiffy reefing system

Now let's look at the whole sequence of events involved in putting in a reef together with the reasons why.

Step	Operation	Reason
1.	Sail close hauled or on a close reach.	So that the mainsail can de-power.
2.	Tension the topping lift.	To support the boom.
3.	Ease the kicker and the mainsheet.	To de-power the mainsail and let the boom lift.
4.	Lower the sail, hook the reef cringle over between cowhorn and re-tension the halyard.	To secure the luff.
5.	Pull the reefing pennant tight.	To secure the leech.
6.	Ease the topping lift.	To allow the sail to take its proper shape.
7.	Re-tension the kicker and mainsheet.	To return to sailing.

Shaking out reefs is a reversal of the procedure for putting them in. Always remember to take the weight of the boom on the topping lift before you release the reefing pennant and make sure that there is no strain in the leach of the sail before pulling on the halyard.

CHAPTER 6

SAILING UPWIND

So far we've looked at sails singly but this is rarely the case in reality. Most rigs call for at least two sails; three is common on ketches and cutters, and there could be even more on classic yachts and such oddities as staysail schooners. But, for simplicity's sake, we'll let the modern sloop rig, with its single headsail and mainsail, represent all of these multi-sailed types.

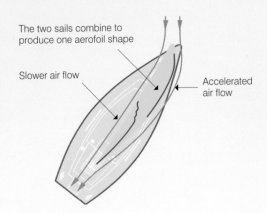

The two sails combine to produce one aerofoil shape

Slower air flow

Accelerated air flow

Acting as one

When sailing close hauled the sails of a fore and aft rigged boat combine to form a single foil. The accelerated air flow around the back of the foresail will attach to the outer surface of the main, while the flow around the inside of the two sails, and in the slot between them, will slow down. For trimming purposes, it therefore makes sense to watch the leading edge (luff) of the foresail for signs of luffing, but not to be so concerned with the luff of the mainsail.

It follows therefore that you should pay particular attention to the outside telltales on the foresail, and ensure that they are all flowing out straight plus the telltales on the mainsail leach. The inside, foresail telltales are bound to lift in the stalled inside air so our concern should only be to have them flying consistently from the bottom to the top of the sail.

Sails – small but perfectly formed

If we accept that the two sails are acting as a single foil when close hauled then the concept of overlapping foresails becomes invalid. What you gain in effective foresail area, you lose in effective mainsail area, so close-hauled sailing is definitely a situation where we can say that small but perfectly formed is best.

Balance is a huge issue when close hauled. A mainsail that's too big for the wind strength will produce more heel, that leads to more weather helm and spoils any chance of achieving a light helm and an easy passage.

For efficient close-hauled sailing start with a 100% genoa as a maximum, and don't be shy about reefing the mainsail if the weather helm increases above five degrees.

Light airs (Force 1 to 2)

In light airs we want to obtain as much power as possible from sails, but if we ask too much of the airflow, the outside air will lose its attachment to the foil surface and become turbulent, stalling the sail.

Let's start setting up the rig from the front:

1 Leave the backstay quite slack to allow some forestay sag and produce a fuller foresail. It will also allow more fullness in the mainsail, as the mast will have straightened a little.

2 Keep halyard tensions light to keep the entry angles from increasing too much but accept that you won't be able to sail as close to the wind as you will when the breeze builds.

3 Trim the foresail on tight. But then ease the sheet traveller car back to allow as much twist as the top telltales will allow.

4 Bring the boom to the centreline using the mainsheet and traveller, then ease the clew outhaul slightly to allow a little bit of shape in the lower part of the mainsail.

5 Keeping the boom centred, ease the mainsheet and haul the traveller car to windward to allow as much twist in the mainsail as the top telltale will accept without stalling.

6 In very light conditions move any mobile and co-operative crew weight including the helm to the lower side of the boat. Inducing a little bit of heel will help to stop the sails from flapping and produce a little bit of lift from the underwater foils.

Medium wind (Force 3 to 4)

For most sailing cruisers these will be perfect winds for close-hauled work, and you should be able to sail effectively at the closest possible angles to the wind. Flat sails are the order of the day, to minimise the entry angles.

1 Increase tension in the backstay to take out the forestay sag and bend the mast a little, flattening both sails.

2 Trim on the foresail tight, but with the sheet traveller car further forward to even out the curves in the foot and leach. The telltales should be flying evenly from top to bottom with the outer ribbons flying horizontally and the inner lifting upwards and away from the surface of the sail.

3 With the mainsail, start with the boom on the centreline, then haul on the sheet and kicker to bring the top batten parallel with the boom. Trim on the clew outhaul to flatten the lower part of the sail and increase the halyard tension and/or haul on the Cunningham to take the draft forward and flatten the trailing part of the sail.

4 All of the lower telltales should be flying out straight from the leach but the top one should just be on the point of breaking.

5 Now let the mainsheet traveller down the track to reduce any weather helm to a maximum of five degrees.

6 Get the crew weight to the high side of the boat to reduce heel.

Heavy winds (Force 5 and above)

Heavy wind will increase the forestay sag and fullness of the foresail more than the backstay tensioning system can cope with. It will also kick up a sea state that will need to be negotiated by the helm, making steering a precision course almost impossible. So the more tolerant steering slot you get from having a fuller foresail will be an advantage.

- Applying more tension in the backstay will open the mainsail leach further, de-powering the sail. And you will have to drop the traveller further down the track in order to reduce building weather helm.
- Don't be concerned with luffing in the forward third of the mainsail, but if you are dealing with more than a short gust then it's a good indicator that it's time to reef the mainsail.

Target speeds

Most modern cruising sailboats actually sail very well, and while that is a very good thing it can lead to a problem when sailing close hauled, in that the boats are quite reluctant to stall. I see a lot of instances where helms will have all the telltales doing the right things and the boat looks fine but it isn't really going anywhere. Effectively the helms are sailing on the edge of a stall and although the air is still flowing over the sails in the right direction there is not enough power to develop a proper boat speed and effective progress to windward is poor.

Racers, with their high performance rigs, are used to the problem and many of them will get over it by using a target up-wind boat speed. Here's how it goes! You will need a good idea of the speed that the boat should do, upwind.

Let's say that your target speed is 6 knots. If your speed to windward falls below 6 knots, bear away in five-degree stages, until the speed rises to the right number. Give the boat a good chance to speed up between course changes.

If the boat speed is above 6 knots then close up on the wind until the speed drops to the target. By taking advantage of a course closer to the wind, your effective progress to windward should improve.

Upwind target speeds

True wind speed	True wind angle	Up wind VMG	Target boat speed
6	45	4.26	6.02
8	42	5.01	6.74
10	39	5.45	7.01
12	38	5.72	7.26
14	37	5.89	7.38
16	36	6.00	7.41
20	36	6.10	7.54

Up-wind VMG

Put your up-wind destination into your GPS as a waypoint, and the machine will display your VMG (velocity made good) to the waypoint. You can use the VMG read out instead of a target speed.

At first if you are not sure which is the most effective tack, try both, and see which gives you the best VMG. Once set up in the right direction adjust your angle on the wind to maximise the VMG.

If you use your actual destination as the waypoint the GPS will tell you that the VMG is reducing when you cross a radial line emanating from the waypoint, even if you are on the making tack. It will encourage you to tack down a cone of approach that is not necessarily the most efficient course.

To get around the machine's shortcoming, place your waypoint some 10 miles upwind of your actual destination. You will then get a true VMG reading all the way in. Remember to stop at the destination, not the upwind waypoint!

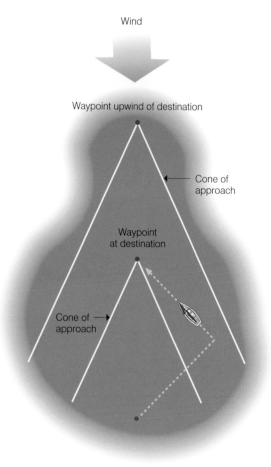

Wind

Waypoint upwind of destination

Cone of approach

Waypoint at destination

Cone of approach

Lee bowing the tide

Should you have to beat across a tide stream, the tack that takes you into the tide will give the best VMG to your destination. Tacking off downstream is tempting because the speed over the ground (SOG) reading will be huge, but it's not a representation of progress towards your destination. So don't be tempted by high SOG numbers. Keep the tide on the lee bow and maximise VMG.

TOP TIP

If you can time your passage to give equal periods of tide stream in each direction, you can tack on the tide change to keep the stream on the leeward bow and achieve the fastest possible up-wind passage.

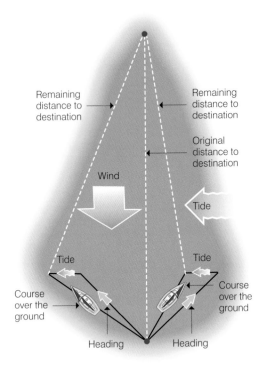

Wind shifts and squalls

Wind is rarely constant in strength or direction and if you are making an up-wind passage in open water there are huge gains to be made in overall progress if you can respond to the shifts. Here are some tips to make the most of them:

- Take a look at a detailed weather forecast before you set off. You can then tack off to be on the correct side of the forecast change in wind direction so that the shift will lift you towards your goal.

- Keep a check on your compass course. If you are headed – that's to say pushed away from your destination – by a wind shift of, say, 15°, then it's time to go about and take advantage of the improvement on the other tack.

- In high pressure, light wind conditions, the shifts often come in waves, with shifts going in opposite directions by 10° or more. If you can tack on the shifts, in phase with the pressure waves, then you can save hours on an up-wind passage.

- Squall clouds can be a real advantage to up-wind progress. Generally, if the cloud looks as though it will pass to the left of your course, tack to the right and enjoy the lift around the cloud. If the cloud will pass to your right then tack to the left for the same effect.

CHAPTER 7

REACHING

After a long period hard on the wind, cracking off onto a reach can be a pure joy. But don't relax – there's lots of work to be done to make the most of this point of sail.

1 First ease the genoa sheet until the outside telltales lift and fly straight while the inside telltales fly straight but lift by 20° or so.

2 Now let the mainsail down the track to ease the pressure on the helm and encourage the bottom couple of leach telltales to fly straight out. Next ease the mainsheet and kicking strap to allow a little more twist, enough to encourage the top leach telltale to fly out straight.

3 Next ease the backstay to straighten the mast, this will make the mainsail fuller and more powerful. It will also introduce some forestay sag making the foresail fuller and more powerful as well.

• Increasing the foresail halyard tension – drags the sail's draft forward and produces a more powerful sail shape coupled with more forward drive.

• Increasing the mainsail halyard tension – pulls the draft of the mainsail forward in the upper part of the sail and pulling on the Cunningham does the same to the lower part. This makes the sail more powerful and encourages forward drive.

• Easing the clew outhaul considerably – makes the mainsail more powerful and enables you to pull trim on the mainsheet while keeping a good entry angle to the wind and opening up the slot between the mainsail and the foresail.

Now let's look at some other ways of keeping that slot open to the benefit of the airflow around both sails.

Tracks and barber haulers

Some larger cruising boats with wide side decks have two parallel genoa traveller tracks. Inner tracks should be used for sailing close-hauled, and outer tracks for reaching.

If you don't have two tracks you can still alter the sheet lead when reaching using a barber hauler, a block which runs on the sheet just in front of the foresail sheet car. It can be used to haul the sheet outboard when reaching to open the slot between foresail and mainsail. Alternatively, it can be used to haul the sheet inboard to decrease the entry angle when working close hauled.

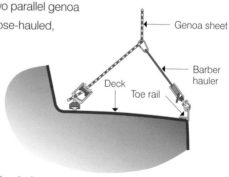

Genoa sheet

Barber hauler

Deck

Toe rail

Reaching blocks

When reaching at 70° to 90° off the wind it pays to run the active (leeward) foresail sheet outside the guard rails and then inboard via a block placed on the toe rail a little aft of the genoa sheet car.

This technique will allow the foresail clew to fly much further to leeward, and open the slot between the foresail and the mainsail.

Running a third sheet through the reaching block will save a lot of re-running of the original sheets, and make it easier to come closer to the wind.

Leave original sheet in place so that you can return to close reaching without re-rigging

Third change sheet lead outside guard rails through reaching block

Reaching block set up on toe rail

Whisker poles

In downwind sailing, we talk about poling a genoa out to windward, a commonly seen technique. In days gone by it was common to see jibs poled out to leeward. The technique was banned under the Racing Rules but remains a perfectly legitimate way for opening the slot if you're not racing.

It works best with an adjustable pole and a 100% sail with a reasonably high clew. If you attempt the technique with a low cut sail, make sure that the pole end stays well clear of the water even when the boat rolls.

If you use a spinnaker pole use a third jib sheet through the end, leaving the two traditionally run sheets free to use without the need to de-rig the pole.

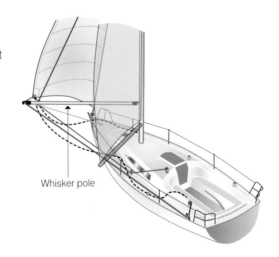

Whisker pole

The jib has been poled out to leeward to open the slot and make the sail more efficient on a broad reach

Reaching sails

Though not so common these days, dedicated reaching sails like the jib top, can be really useful to the cruising skipper with a small crew. The jib top is a foresail with a very full cut, and a high jib cut to the foot. The very high clew allows the sheet to be led well aft (all the way to the quarter) and the clew, therefore, to be flown well outboard, opening the slot between the foresail and mainsail to the maximum.

Jib top foresail

Jib top sheet led all the way aft

Hull speeds

Sailboats can carry a lot of sail when reaching but it doesn't make sense to overdo it. Once a displacement boat reaches its hull speed (the maximum speed that the hull can be pushed through the water) any further effort or energy will only produce heeling and excessive pressure on the helm.

You will know when the hull speed has been reached, since the bow wave will be as far forward as it can go and the stern wave will be at the transom. Pushing the boat any harder will cause the stern to drop into the trough between them, creating more drag.

If, say, you have reached your boat's hull speed of 8 knots, don't push for yet more speed. Instead, de-power the sails or even reduce sail area to provide a balanced, easy ride. You are better off sailing easy at 7.9 knots than fighting the helm at 8.1.

CHAPTER 8

DOWNWIND SAILING

Downwind sailing should be a pleasure in all conditions, yet many sailors turn it into a rolling or gybing nightmare for the sake of a couple of extra lines and safety devices. So let's look at a couple of methods for making sure that those sleigh rides remain pleasurable.

Preventers

If you run with a mainsail up for any length of time, rig a preventer. It won't stop you from gybing accidentally – that's down to the skill of the helm – but it will prevent the damage to gear and crew caused by the boom and mainsheet flying violently across the cockpit.

They are very simple to rig. Take a line from the end of the boom, pass it around a strong point well forward on the boat and then return it into the cockpit where it can be tightened and made fast. The illustration shows the red preventer line has been clipped to the boom end and then turned around the forward deck cleat before returning to a halyard winch on the cabin top. There's more than one way to rig a preventer but I like the system shown for two reasons:

1 Returning the line to the cockpit means you can release it quickly if you need to gybe or to close up on the wind.

2 Attaching it to the boom end ensures that the boom is supported if the end dips in the water on a heavy roll. Lines attached part way down the boom will produce an eccentric load that may lead to a broken boom if the end catches a wave.

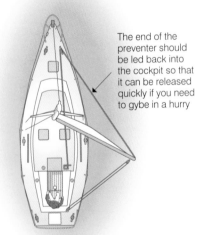

The end of the preventer should be led back into the cockpit so that it can be released quickly if you need to gybe in a hurry

TOP TIP

If you tie the preventer to the boom, use a long loop and a bowline, so that you can reach the knot from the deck without having to centre the mainsail.

Rigging a preventer will stop the boom flying across the cockpit if you gybe accidentally

Poling out headsails

When running or on a very deep broad reach, jibs and genoas are bound to set poorly in the mainsail's wind shadow. However, you can spread the headsail to windward – called goosewinging – or wing on wing – out of the mainsail wind shadow so the air flow across the sail will be reversed, from leach to luff, and it will set very effectively.

Goosewinging using the headsail sheet alone will only work for a few degrees above a dead run – and even then the sail will set and collapse repeatedly – but if the sail is sheeted through the end of a spinnaker pole, or whisker pole, the arrangement works well for winds from dead aft to about 40° off the run.

The result will be a worthwhile improvement in boat speed as well as a nicely balanced feel to the helm. What's more, adding a couple of extra control lines will not compromise your ability to tack or gybe the boat quickly.

In *fig 57,* the spinnaker pole has been set up normally with a downhaul (yellow) and an uphaul, or topping lift, (green). An extra back guy (blue) has been added and led aft. This will stop the pole from swinging forwards when the sheet is released. An extra sheet (red) has been tied to the sail's clew and led through the end of the spinnaker pole to a block at the quarter and then to a winch.

You can see that the jib is setting well on its third (red) sheet, but, importantly, this sheet can be released at any time leaving the sail to be controlled normally using its two standard sheets.

If the pole and gear were to foul the headsail when trimmed for a close haul, then the downhaul and back guy can be released and the pole pulled vertically against the mast using the uphaul.

So as long as you take the trouble to rig a back guy and a third sheet you can sail on any point of sailing without the need to de-rig.

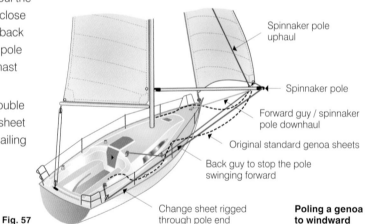

Spinnaker pole uphaul

Spinnaker pole

Forward guy / spinnaker pole downhaul

Original standard genoa sheets

Back guy to stop the pole swinging forward

Change sheet rigged through pole end

Poling a genoa to windward

Fig. 57

Roll control

Rolling from side to side, particularly coupled with a moderate or rough sea state, is very uncomfortable and tiring. It can be dangerous for crew trying to move around below and in particular if it induces a chinese gybe – an accidental gybe when the mast rolls to windward.

Most of the rolling is caused by excessive twist in sails. If the leach at the top of the sails is allowed to twist forward of the beam, the flow of air will be directed upwards and outwards, driving the mast top sideways. To stop the rolling you need to straighten your leaches by pulling down on the mainsail kicker (vang) and taking the foresail sheet leads forward.

Mainsail or no mainsail?

Downwind sailing is tough on mainsails. When eased enough to run safely, they often chafe on spreaders and rigging. More significant is their effect on the boat. With a large amount of sail area set well outboard, they have a tendency to turn the boat towards the wind – enough to cause broaching if the wind and sea state builds.

In many circumstances it makes sense to drop the main and let the wind get to your genoa. Some sailors will argue that sailing under genoa or jib alone will compromise your ability to sail upwind, but that doesn't really apply to modern rigs. The fact that the mainsail is flaked nicely on the boom can be a relief in many circumstances – particularly when the breeze builds.

Training runs – tacking downwind

You can work your way downwind comfortably without the use of spinnaker poles and extra rigging and with two sails working effectively. Sail a broad reach close to your desired course – just close enough to the wind for the genoa to set. Make sure that you are staying in safe water, and then be prepared to gybe onto the opposite broad reach to re-cross your downwind course. Work your way downwind in a series of broad reaching zigzags safe from the threat of an imminent accidental gybe.

1 To set up the most advantageous reaching angle, start from a near run and then slowly turn towards the wind until the jib or genoa sets properly.

2 As the foresail sets, you will feel an immediate increase in speed. Trim both sails to best effect, starting with the foresail and settle in to a fast reach.

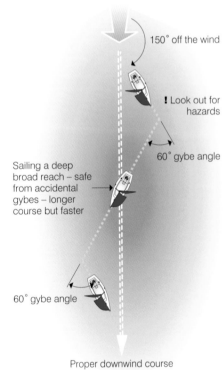

150° off the wind

! Look out for hazards

60° gybe angle

Sailing a deep broad reach – safe from accidental gybes – longer course but faster

60° gybe angle

Proper downwind course

Tacking downwind

TOP TIP

The best reaching angle will probably prove to be 150° or so off of the true wind direction, so when planning the next gybe look for a gybe angle of about 60°.

Downwind VMG

VMG (velocity made good) is the effective speed towards your destination.

The most efficient, and fastest, point of sailing is a beam reach and a dead run is inefficient in sail trim terms, therefore slow. So it stands to reason that the most efficient downwind course lies somewhere between those two courses. But how do you find that perfect angle where the VMG towards your destination is maximised?

- First put a waypoint at your destination into the GPS and ask the machine to read distance and bearing to the waypoint. Then, starting just off a run slowly turn towards the wind watching the boat speed and the VMG shown on the GPS rise.

- Sail the bearing that gives the maximum VMG and hold that heading until you reach the gybe point that will give the equivalent opposite heading into the waypoint.

In *fig 59a*, the helm has increased boat speed from 4 knots to 6 knots by turning upwind by 30° onto a more efficient broad reach. Though the boat has turned away from the direct route to the destination the VMG has increased to 5.2 knots, so they will get there sooner.

In still waters, and if your waypoint is dead downwind, you could take off to the right or left of the direct line to the waypoint without a care. If there's a cross-current, however, there's no choice to make. You should take off into the flow which will push you back towards the destination without any loss of boat speed – so the VMG will be even better, *(fig 59b)*.

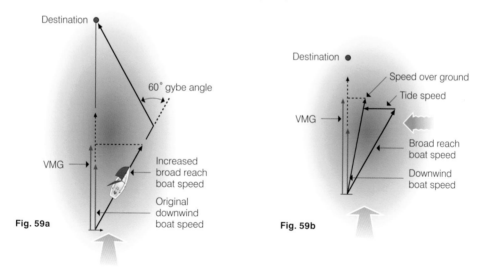

Fig. 59a

Fig. 59b

Using waves and gusts

When you start to surf on a wave or when hit by a gust, the boat will accelerate. The surge of speed will send the 'apparent wind' forward, reducing the sails' entry angles. A good helm will bear away, progressively, as the speed increases, keeping the entry angles constant and the sails working efficiently. Of course, you must be prepared to 'head up' again when the boat slows at the bottom of the wave, or when the gust eases.

CHAPTER 9

TRADE WIND SAILING

Bowling down the trades with the wind from over your quarter, a high boat speed and the expectation of a rum punch on a tropical island is the stuff of many sailors' dreams.

But the real skill involved in bowling down the trades for days on end is not about keeping up a good boat speed, it's about maintaining a stable working platform and living space, while minimising chafe and wear (on the boat and the crew!).

Potential wear points on the sails are easy to see. Any place where the sail has to rub on a stanchion or safety rail you should put reinforced wear patches on the sail plus padding on the wear surface. Potential wear points in the running rigging are, however, much harder to see but will be happening insidiously everywhere that a rope turns a sheave, runs through a clutch or just lays over a wire.

There are a few steps that are easy to take to minimise the chances of ropes wearing through:

- You can leave halyards on winches or secured on cleats rather than use jamming cleats or compression clutches that will shred the outer braiding.

- Use bowlines instead of shackles to secure sheets, guys and halyards to sails. If you re-tie them every couple of days using a different position for the knot, all of the wear points on that particular rope will move along the line. You can turn sheets and guys end for end every now and then, again to move the wear points along the rope.

- Where sheets or guys pass through the end fittings on spinnaker or whisker poles there can be a lot of friction wear, so tie a length of sacrificial rope to the end of your proper racing sheet and let that take the wear.

Some classic wear points to look out for:

1 Where the genoa foot will lay across the safety rails.

2 Close to the mainsail headboard where the main halyard will wear against the edge of the sheave box when the main is eased a lot.

3 Where the mainsail lies against the spreaders when it's eased to the maximum.

Twin Headsails

If you're going to be running, or broad reaching for a while, take down the mainsail and let your largest genoa go to work. If you want to increase the working sail area, set an additional jib poled out to windward. The second jib can be set up loose luffed (meaning it isn't hanked to a stay) but be sure to fit a second lazy sheet to the sail, and a back stay to the pole to make sail recovery easier and prevent the pole from swinging forward.

There are other variations on this theme. Most foresail or roller reefing foils have a pair of tracks and it's possible to run a sail up each. With one sail setting naturally to leeward and the other poled out to windward you have a tremendously effective sail area, giving good balance without any risk of accidental gybes. By laying the windward sail inside the leeward one you can roll both sails away together, either to reduce sail or stow them.

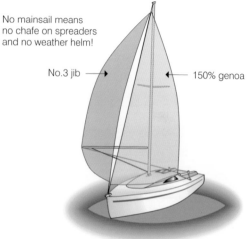

No mainsail means no chafe on spreaders and no weather helm!

No.3 jib →   ← 150% genoa

TOP TIP

Whenever you set twin foresails remember to close down the leaches of both sails to avoid rolling.

This boat has its 150% genoa set normally to leeward and a jib set loose luffed and poled out to windward.
Always set up a loose luffed sail with a lazy sheet that can be hauled on when recovering the sail!

Some boats intended for trade wind sailing are equipped with twin forestays set close together and inline fore and aft. Both forestays can have roller reefing gears, carrying furling genoas, or plain wire for hanked on sails. Others have traditional inner forestays and staysails, or an inner forestay that's stowed by the shrouds when not needed, but can then be rigged and tensioned in an instant by means of a highfield lever.

In any case, two large genoas set wing on wing and coupled with two spinnaker poles produces a powerful, easily controlled and well balanced downwind sail plan. The sort of sail plan that leaves the helmsman time to dream of white beaches, rum punch and...

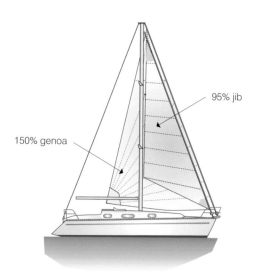

95% jib

150% genoa

This boat has two foresails set on twin forestays each with roller furling gear – ideal for a bowling down the trade winds!

CHAPTER 10

SPINNAKERS

Spinnakers in their various guises can induce panic and fear among sailors. Indeed, many of us have experienced moments of terror when our boats have broached heavily, leaving us clinging to the deck while the rig shakes and the spinnaker shreds in the water alongside. But those moments are few and far between and generally occur on the racecourse when, frankly, boats are being pushed too hard. For every one of those scary moments I have spent hours and hours cruising on a broad reach in light winds, a spinnaker pulling us along nicely, and with no more than my wife and two children on board.

The fact is that racers get into trouble because they sail with their spinnakers on a beam reach or in too much wind. So my advice to cruising skippers is – only use a spinnaker in light breezes and when running or broad reaching!

If you keep the spinnaker up for too long, as the breeze rises in strength, it will become increasingly troublesome when it becomes time to drop it. As with all forms of sail reduction – do it early, perhaps adopting one of the other techniques we discussed in Chapter 8, such as poling out a genoa to windward.

When beam reaching with a spinnaker you will find that very small increases in boat speed or wind strength will result in sudden and large pressure increases in the sail. This can lead to uncontrollable weather helm and broaching – a distinctly unpleasant experience! Actually, most sailing cruisers on a beam reach will go faster with a genoa than a spinnaker and with a lot less weather helm. So keep the spinnaker below decks until you are committed to a long broad reach.

TOP TIP

Only use a spinnaker in light breezes and when running or broad reaching.

Asymmetric spinnakers

Also called cruising chutes and gennakers. A loose luffed headsail, tacked ahead of the forestay, with a half width greater than 75% of the foot and no battens. I guess that the name changes to suit the customer, but for now, we'll go with gennaker.

Gennakers will give your downwind performance a boost compared with that of a genoa, but not quite the boost or flexibility of a symmetrical spinnaker. They are, however, a lot easier to sail with, requiring less gear and fewer hands to operate.

But you will need some extra gear:

- A spinnaker halyard to start with and then

- Two sheets, each about two and a half times the length of the boat. The sheets will lead from the clew of the sail outside everything via turning blocks on the quarters to convenient winches in the cockpit – cockpit-mounted halyard winches will often do.

- Lastly you will need a tack line which needs to run forward from the cockpit, via a system of organisers, to a block fitted to the stem head or bowsprit ahead of the forestay, then to the tack of the sail. To be able to recover the sail completely and easily, the tack line will need to be around twice the boat's length.

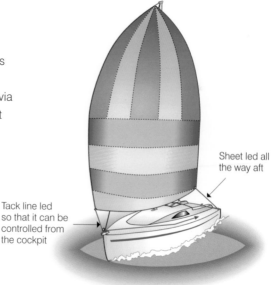

Sheet led all the way aft

Tack line led so that it can be controlled from the cockpit

Asymmetric spinnaker, cruising chute or gennaker

Setting a gennaker

1 Sail on a broad reach with the foresail still set. Bring the gennaker on deck and clip the bag to the leeward rails with the tack nearest the bow. Open the bag and pull the three corners of the sail to the top.

2 Bring the leeward sheet forward, outside the active genoa sheet, under the genoa and over the guardrails, attaching it to the clew of the sail.

3 Bring the windward sheet forward outside the forestay, under the genoa and over the guardrails attaching it to the clew.

4 Bring the tack line from the stemhead block, under the genoa, (but over the guardrails) and attach it to the tack of the gennaker sail.

5 Finally bring the halyard from outside, (under the genoa) and over the guardrails to an attachment with the head of the sail. You are now ready to hoist.

Hoisting

1 When you are ready for the hoist, pull on the tack line until the tack of the sail is about 1 metre (3 feet) from the stemhead block then secure it.

2 Next take the sheet and, leaving plenty of slack, put a couple of turns around the winch and secure it.

3 Now take a good look around to make sure that all's clear and also that conditions have not changed.

4 Next, hoist the sail quickly to the top of the mast and secure the halyard. The sail will probably be hanging limp behind the genoa now so try turning gently to windward to see if the sail lifts. If it does, all well and good, stow the genoa and enjoy the sail. If it still hangs limply roll away or drop the genoa and try again. The sail should lift and fill now so be prepared for a surge of weather helm as it does.

Trimming

Once the gennaker has set and you're back on course, ease the sheet until the sail's luff starts to curl then trim back a little bit. If the luff hasn't curled for a while ease the sheet again until it does.

It's a continuous process and potentially tiring but don't slacken. If the sail is trimmed on too far (very common) then the boat will not only go slower but you will develop more weather helm making the steering heavier and harder.

Reaching

If you want to turn upwind a little towards a reach, pull in the tack line to straighten the luff and make the sail swing to leeward of the bow. Then trim on the sheet to suit.

Running

If you turn away from the wind, ease the tack line and the sheet and allow the sail to lift and swing to windward giving lots more forward drive and less heel.

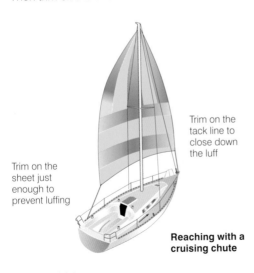

Trim on the tack line to close down the luff

Trim on the sheet just enough to prevent luffing

Reaching with a cruising chute

Ease the tack line to allow the sail to fly out to windward

Ease the sheet to keep the luff on the point of folding

Running with a cruising chute

Gybing

Gybing a gennaker is very straightforward.

1 First sail on a very broad reach, easing the mainsheet and the gennaker tack line.

2 Next, pull hard on the lazy gennaker sheet, pulling the clew through the gap between the forestay and tack line.

3 Now complete the mainsail gybe and trim on the new leeward gennaker sheet.

Many skippers will deploy a roller genoa part way before gybing to ensure that the gennaker cannot wrap around the forestay.

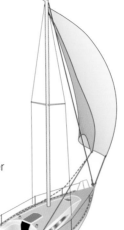

Gybe the sail inside itself but outside the forestay

Before gybing, run deep and pull the clew in past the forestay with the new sheet – then complete the gybe

Dropping

• For an easy drop, always bear away onto a very broad reach and ease the mainsheet so that the mainsail blankets the gennaker. Post one crew on deck as gatherer and have them pull on the lazy gennaker sheet to bring the clew towards them.

• Make a decision whether you want to stuff the sail down the companionway or the forward hatch, then ease the tack line completely and also the active sheet. The sail will now be de-powered behind the mainsail and can be lowered as fast as the gatherer can handle it.

Rollers

Round the world solo racers have had the ability to roll away their code zeros and asymmetric spinnakers, and this technology is now finding its way into the cruising market.

If you don't like the idea of hoisting and dropping your gennaker conventionally then you can buy the extra kit and have a roll away version.

Basically the sail rolls around a lightweight plastic stay operated by a ratchet wheel and a continuous loop of line. The whole arrangement can be hoisted on the spinnaker halyard and tack line then be deployed or rolled away at will. The sausage of sail can then be stowed, rolled below decks.

Bowsprits

There's no doubt that bowsprits improve the performance of asymmetric spinnakers. The addition of even a short bowsprit will push the luff of the sail forward into cleaner air, improve the lift characteristics of the sail and greatly reduce the potential generation of weather helm.

Many producers of modern cruisers and cruiser racers have followed J Yachts' lead and fitted retractable bowsprits to good effect. But they need not be so sophisticated and several spar manufacturers now market retro-fit bowsprit kits for medium sized family cruisers.

Snuffers

Spinnaker snuffers, or socks can be used on all types of spinnaker. They are essentially tubes of ripstop nylon attached to the head of the spinnaker that can be pulled down over the sail, squeezing it into a neat sausage shape. You should bear away so the sail can be snuffed in the lee of the mainsail.

Commonly used by short handed sailors some of whom will snuff their spinnakers before a gybe and then deploy them again afterwards.

I've also seen a spinnaker on a catamaran being used half squeezed in heavy winds to produce a reefed spinnaker.

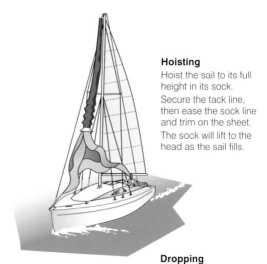

Hoisting
Hoist the sail to its full height in its sock.
Secure the tack line, then ease the sock line and trim on the sheet.
The sock will lift to the head as the sail fills.

Dropping
Ease the sheet and haul on the sock line.
Once the sail is secure in its sock it can be lowered to the deck.

Using a spinnaker sock

Packing spinnakers

Is much simpler than you may think. Spinnakers are rarely folded, but usually stuffed into a bag however it's essential that the sail is not twisted so here is what to do.

1 Have somebody hold the head of the sail, then run your hands down each leach (luff and leach if it's asymmetric) making sure that the seams don't cross over.

2 When you reach the clews (clew and tack on an asymmetric) take them to meet the head.

3 Hold a clew on each side of the head and hold on tight to those three corners.

4 Stuff all of the sail into the bag trying to put the middle in first.

If you're using a standard sail bag, keep the three corners together and tie them in with the draw string. If you are using a rectangular spinnaker bag, tie the head into the tabs in the middle of the bag and the two clews into the tabs at each end.

CHAPTER 11

SYMMETRICAL SPINNAKERS

To fly a traditional symmetrical spinnaker you will need the following extra gear:

1 Spinnaker pole with a fitting on the mast to secure the inboard end. The pole will hold the windward clew of the sail out into the wind.

2 An uphaul running from the outboard end of the pole into the mast at least three quarters of the way up to the top. The control end should be led back to the cockpit. The uphaul will hold the pole end up and provide pole height adjustment.

3 A downhaul, again running from the pole end to a block in the middle of the foredeck and then back to the cockpit. The downhaul, when tensioned, will stop the pole from lifting.

4 A spinnaker sheet for each side of the boat, run outside the rigging and guard rails to a block near the quarter, and then to the cockpit. The sheets should be attached to the clews with quick release shackles. The sheets will be used to control whichever is the leeward clew of the spinnaker.

5 A guy for each side of the boat attached to the sheets near the sail's clews and then run to the cockpit via a block on the side deck or on the gunwale, just forward of the cockpit. The guys will be used to pull the pole end back and forward to adjust the spinnaker's entry angle to the wind.

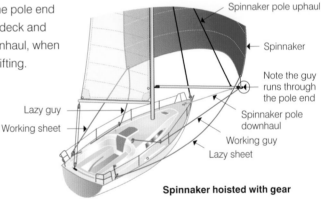

Spinnaker pole uphaul

Spinnaker

Note the guy runs through the pole end

Spinnaker pole downhaul

Working guy

Lazy sheet

Lazy guy

Working sheet

Spinnaker hoisted with gear

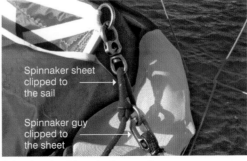

Spinnaker sheet clipped to the sail

Spinnaker guy clipped to the sheet

Spinnaker sheet / guy / sail connection.

Setting up

Let's assume that you are sailing on a broad reach, starboard tack. The spinnaker will be flown on the port side while the pole will be set up to starboard.

1 Bring the spinnaker on deck and clip the bag to the leeward guard rails so that the starboard clew is towards the front of the boat and the port clew towards the back.

2 Bring the port spinnaker sheet and guy (already clipped together), outside the active genoa sheet, over the guard rails and under the genoa to the spinnaker. Clip the port sheet to the port spinnaker clew.

3 Bring the starboard spinnaker sheet and guy (already clipped together) outside of the forestay, over the guard rails, under the genoa and clip the starboard sheet to the starboard spinnaker clew.

4 Attach the inboard end of the pole to the fitting on the mast and attach the uphaul and downhaul to the pole.

5 With the outboard end of the pole still on the deck, clip in the starboard guy on the windward side of the forestay.

6 Lastly bring the spinnaker halyard from outside, under the genoa, over the guardrails and clip it to the head of the spinnaker.

You are now ready for the hoist!

7 Leave the genoa up until the spinnaker has set, this prevents the spinnaker wrapping around the forestay as it's hoisted.

The windward and leeward sheets and guys are attached to the spinnaker clews and the halyard has been attached to the sail's head.

Note that the bag is clipped firmly to the rails so that it won't be launched with the sail.

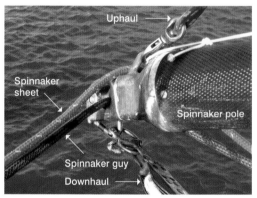

Note that only the active windward guy runs through the pole.

TOP TIP

A useful trick is to hoist spinnakers in stops (meaning that it's bound into a three-legged shape) using wool or elastic bands. The bands will prevent the sail filling while you hoist and will then burst when the sheet is trimmed.

Hoisting

Let's look at a sequence for hoisting the spinnaker, we'll assume that the spinnaker has already been prepared on the foredeck.

1 Sail off on a broad reach, easing the mainsail to the appropriate position but trimming on the foresail to stop it flapping around.

2 Set up the spinnaker pole horizontally, using the pole uphaul, on the windward side of the boat with the spinnaker guy led through the outboard pole end.

3 Trim on the spinnaker guy, bringing the clew of the spinnaker to the pole end and then pull the pole back to about 30° from the centreline and forestay. Load the guy onto the windward primary winch and cleat it. Take up some tension on the pole downhaul. Leaving plenty of slack, load the spinnaker sheet loosely around its winch and cleat it so that you don't lose the end when the sail flaps.

You are now ready to hoist so take another look around and make sure that you have plenty of sea room downwind and that neither the wind speed nor the wind direction have changed.

1 All clear! Hoist the sail quickly to the top of the mast and secure the halyard.

2 By easing the downhaul and trimming on the guy, pull the pole back until it lines up with the boom.

3 Trim on the sheet gently until the sail lifts and sets. Once it sets, ease away on the sheet until the leeward shoulder of the sail just starts to curl.

4 Now is the moment to roll away or drop the foresail.

5 Lastly look at the two clew heights. Remember that the sail is symmetrical so the clew heights should be the same. Adjust the height of the pole end (and windward clew) using the uphaul and downhaul to match it with the height of the leeward clew.

Trimming

When perfectly trimmed, the spinnaker should be just on the edge of collapse. Ease the sheet until the windward shoulder of the sail starts to curl and then trim back a couple of inches. A racing crew will ease and trim continuously to keep the sail working to the optimum despite the constant subtle changes in wind direction, whether caused by nature or the acceleration of the boat. Cruising yachtsmen, however, won't be able to keep up that regime for long, but don't give up, let the helmsman take the strain. When the sail starts to curl at the windward shoulder steer off wind by 10° or so. Then, when the sail has settled, gently steer back to windward until the curling starts.

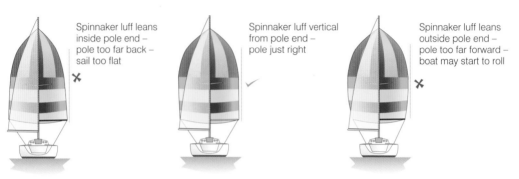

Spinnaker luff leans inside pole end – pole too far back – sail too flat

Spinnaker luff vertical from pole end – pole just right

Spinnaker luff leans outside pole end – pole too far forward – boat may start to roll

Spinnaker trim – pole position

Guy trim, or pole position is important if the sail is to be settled and docile. If the pole is too far forward then the windward edge of the sail will lean out from the pole end. If the pole is too far back it will lean in, and if it is just right the edge will be vertical from the end of the pole.

If curling occurs near to the head of the spinnaker then the pole is probably too high. If curling occurs low down near the clew then the pole is probably too low. Curling should occur right on the shoulder of the sail.

It's well worth putting effort into spinnaker trim. A well trimmed sail will be stable and easy on the crew. If the sail is twisted it will be very hard to trim and may well start an unwelcome rolling motion in the boat.

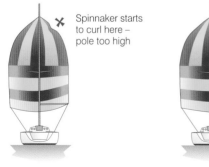

Spinnaker starts to curl here – pole too high

Spinnaker starts to curl here – pole too low!

Spinnaker starts to curl here – pole height just right – sail clews are level

Spinnaker trim – pole heights

Gybing – dip pole method

The dip pole method is usually for larger yachts and those without fixed inner forestays. To perform the gybe you need somebody to steer the boat, somebody to operate the sheets, guys, uphaul and downhaul in the cockpit and somebody on the foredeck to swing the pole and engage the new guy.

Let's go through the process step by step:

1 Sail on a very broad reach.

2 Take all of the slack out of the lazy sheet and secure it.

3 Trip the pole from the active guy and lower the outboard end to the deck.

4 Make both guys slack while keeping the spinnaker flying using the two sheets.

5 Gybe the mainsail and settle on the opposite very broad reach.

6 Swing the pole through the fore triangle and clip in the new guy.

7 Hoist the pole to the horizontal then trim the new guy to bring the pole end back to align with the boom.

8 Let go the windward sheet and trim the spinnaker using the leeward sheet.

9 Take up slack in the downhaul and sail away!

Don't be tempted to gybe from a beam reach to a beam reach, it's a sure-fire way of wrapping the sail around the forestay. Always run and square the pole back before the gybe. When flying the spinnaker on the two sheets don't be too disappointed if the sail flaps. Just make sure that the two clews are in front of the forestay to avoid the twisting action that will start the sail wrapping.

Gybing – end to end method

If a yacht has a fixed inner forestay the dip pole method is impossible because the pole cannot swing past the stay. In this circumstance, and on many smaller yachts, the end to end method is the method of choice. Most of the method of gybing is common to both methods – it's just the way that the two guys are transferred at the pole end that differs. An end to end pole will have common fittings at both ends and the uphauls and downhauls will be attached at the middle of the pole usually with rope yokes.

Let's look at the steps involved in the method:

1 Sail on a very broad reach.

2 Take the slack out of the lazy sheet and secure it.

3 Trip the active guy from the pole end.

4 Trip the inboard pole end from the mast, swing it forward of the inner forestay, and clip in the new guy.

5 Gybe the mainsail and sail on the opposite very broad reach.

6 Swing the old outboard pole end forward of the inner forestay and clip it to the mast.

7 Trim on the new guy and sail away.

You may need to ease the downhaul during the operation to provide enough movement in the pole, but keep the uphaul set so the foredeck crew don't have to hold the pole up.

Many small boats will work a spinnaker with just a sheet on each clew of the sail. The same line will act as a sheet to leeward and as a guy when to windward. These boats will usually fit twinning lines or barber haulers at the widest beam to pull a guy downwards and provide better pole control.

Boats operating with both sheets and guys on both sides will still use twinning lines, both to adjust the alignment of a sheet to the spinnaker and fine tune sail shape. In strong winds you can pull down on the pole end and the twinning line to leeward to pull in the spinnaker leaches, de-power the sail a little and reduce the risk of rolling.

Spinnaker sheet

These twinning lines can be used to adjust the lead sheet angle.

Dropping – by the head

For an easy spinnaker drop, always bear away onto a very broad reach and ease the mainsheet so the spinnaker will drop in the lee of the mainsail. Then hoist the foresail so that the spinnaker cannot twist around the forestay on its way down. You have to decide where you are going to store the sail – either down the main companionway and into the saloon or through a forward hatch into the forward cabin.

1 If you go for the forward hatch option, put one crew in the forecabin and pass them the lazy guy having run it over the guard rails and under the foresail. Their job will be to pull on the lazy guy and then the spinnaker to bring the whole sail into the cabin as it drops.

2 Next, ease the pole forward until it's just short of the forestay and then trim the sheet on tight. Prepare the halyard for dropping.

3 When you're ready, drop the halyard about 2 metres (6 feet) very quickly. With the foot pulled tight the head of the sail will fall away and spill wind.

4 As the wind spills from the sail let go the sheet, then the guy, and start pulling the sail into the boat. Control the drop with the halyard to keep the sail out of the water.

Dropping – tripping the windward clew

Again bear away onto a very broad reach and ease the mainsheet.

1 Take the lazy guy and this time hand it over the rails to a crew member standing in the companionway.

2 Ease the spinnaker pole forward and down until the pole end is within easy reach of a crew member on the foredeck.

3 Trip the spinnaker from the sheet at the pole end. Don't stand with your head behind the pole when tripping! The pole will spring back with the release of pressure.

4 The sail will now fly out flag-like behind the mainsail and can be gathered into the companionway.

5 Drop the sail slowly with the halyard, giving the crew time to keep it out of the water.

Broaching

An uncontrolled turn into the wind and is to be avoided! If you sail too close to the wind, weather helm will build very quickly, and may overpower the rudder. If you accelerate quickly for instance when surfing, the apparent wind will move forward and you will end up with the same effect – too much weather helm and loss of steerage.

To avoid a broach, ease sheets and bear away from the wind as soon as you sense the weather helm building up pressure on the rudder. Bearing away, keeping the boat level and under, the sail should take the pressure off the helm.

If you can't sail your course comfortably with an easy pressure on the helm then it's time to take the spinnaker down!

If you do broach, don't panic! The flogging sails and shaking rig – not to mention the unusual amount of heel – can be scary. You must de-power both sails by easing sheets and opening the kicker – centring the helm so the rudder can start to work again. Then, as the boat comes upright and starts to move ahead, bear away from the wind and trim on. You probably won't encounter much argument from the crew if you decide to take the spinnaker down then!

CHAPTER 12

SAILS AND SAILCLOTHS

Even the best sails wear out. When the leach of your favourite genoa splits every time you tack, or when you finally admit that you can't pull the draft of the sail forward any less than 60% of the chord length, you'll know it's time to visit your sailmaker.

But, just like the first time you stepped onto a boat, you're faced with a whole new language when you walk into a sail loft. But don't worry, all sailmakers' terms are contained in the glossary on page 75.

When choosing sails, it's important to have an understanding of the properties, good and bad, of the many different fibres on offer. Stronger fibres give the sailmaker the opportunity to produce lighter sails of an adequate strength and lighter sails mean less heel, improved stability, etc. but at what cost?

Here's my view on the pros and cons of the main types of sail fibres:

Nylon Particularly good at shock absorbing and weaves well with a good finish. Not good UV resistance.

PET Polyester (DACRON®): Good UV resistance and flex characteristics these fibres weave well with a good finish. No cons but a very low modulus means that you need a lot of fibres to produce a non-stretch fabric.

PEN Polyester (PENTEX®): Good UV resistance and flex, with 40% less stretch than PET Polyester. Doesn't weave as well, so cloth is impregnated with resin filler. Low cost fibre for use in laminates.

Vectran® (liquid crystal polymer): A medium modulus fibre with excellent flex life, very expensive and has poor UV resistance.

Kevlar® / Twaron® (aramid): excellent all round performance but limited UV resistance and flex life.

Spectra® / Dyneema® (modified polyethylene): good flex characteristics and UV resistance with lower stretch than the aramids. They are subject to creep however.

PBO (extremely high modulus fibre): Very low stretch fibres and very expensive, low UV resistance and low flex life.

Carbon (extremely high modulus fibre): Very low stretch, good UV resistance but very low flex life.

Now you have an understanding of the materials available, you need to analyse just what you want from your sails. I guess we'd all like sails that are lightweight, non-stretch, strong, UV resistant, capable of being stuffed into a small bag without deterioration and with a working life roughly equivalent to our own. But, as far as I'm aware, that sail material isn't available, yet!

A cruising sailor's sail wardrobe will be limited, so sails need to be effective across a range of conditions, they need to be stowed in small spaces and handled by relatively weak crews. So the choice of sail material will centre on the way that the sails can be handled, rather than their optimum performance when sailing.

Then there's their weight. On a small to medium sized cruising yacht – up to 40 feet (12 metres) – crew sizes tend to be smaller and sail stowage more limited than on a larger vessel. The individual sails are relatively compact so they can still be dragged by one man, or carried by two even when made from the heaviest polyester. The overall weight of the individual sails is therefore not so much of a concern. On the other hand, the owner of a 50 footer (15 metres) with a heavy polyester mainsail might need the assistance of four crew just to carry the sail on board and is much more likely to consider a lightweight sail material in the future. So, boat size is another factor when choosing sails.

Laminates

Laminated sailcloths are made up of a core scrim, usually made of high modulus fibres that give the material its strength, bonded between two plies of clear polyester film. Cruising laminates are usually covered with taffeta – a loosely woven polyester cloth – for increased wear resistance.

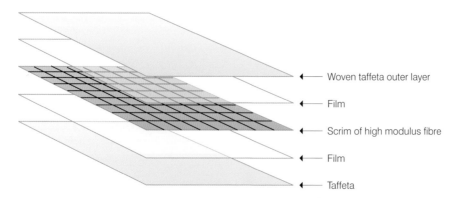

Woven taffeta outer layer

Film

Scrim of high modulus fibre

Film

Taffeta

Construction of cruising laminate sail cloth

Laminate cloths are lightweight and high strength. They keep their shape well and don't distort in the long or short term. The perfect sail cloth then? Well, not for cruising yachtsmen. Laminate sails need more careful handling than most cruisers can give. They need to be carefully rolled or flaked, or the film and glues will break down, flaking off and leaving you with little more than the scrim.

Taffeta covered laminates are more durable but are marginally heavier and require a degree of care that's not easy to achieve on a small boat.

Woven sailcloths

Of the fibres listed, only Vectran® and polyester have the flexibility to weave successfully. Vectran has the higher modulus of the two and will produce a lighter cloth of a given strength than polyester. Unfortunately, it's more expensive and less resistant to UV light.

Woven polyester (often called Dacron®) is the most common sailcloth, but there are many variations in the way that fibres are woven. Polyester, we should remember, has a relatively low modulus – it's quite stretchy. So it takes more fibres, and therefore more weight, to produce a given strength of cloth.

The quality of the sailcloth is crucial. A cheap sailcloth, woven with thick fibres to gain the necessary strength, will have a lot of crimp and therefore a poor balance of directional strength. To compensate, the cloth manufacturer probably smoothes out the rough finish of the cloth with a resin filler. As the cloth flexes, the filler fails and falls out, leaving the high points of the crimped fibres exposed. Woven polyester cloths normally fail across the crimped fibres so expect your sails to rip parallel to the leach and foot of a sail.

Better quality woven sailcloths are made from many finer (high denier) fibres producing a higher tenacity cloth with much less crimp. Less crimp means better balance and a smoother cloth needing much less filler.

TOP TIP

Don't always be swayed by cost. A better cloth will make a better sail that most importantly, will last longer and could prove much the better value in the long run.

UV Protection

All sails are degraded by UV (ultra violet) light and some fibres suffer more than others, and that characteristic alone may affect your choice of sailcloth for different applications.

So you need to protect your sails from sunlight. The best protection involves taking them down when you finish sailing, folding them neatly and stowing them in a dark place, however this is not practical for many owners. Many mainsails will be left flaked on the boom through a whole season and if that's the way that you leave your mainsail then make sure that the mainsail cover actually covers the whole sail and is resistant to the passage of UV light.

Rolling genoas that are left wound on the forestay for long periods must also be well protected, most achieve this protection with the addition of a UV resistant strip – often known as a sacrificial strip – sewn along the leach and foot of the sail. Before leaving the boat make sure that the genoa is wound up tightly and neatly, so that the UV strip completely covers the sail.

In conclusion, I would say that woven polyester sails made of a good quality cloth are the best choice for the cruising yachtsman. They will accept the rough handling on small boats better than those made of more exotic materials. The low modulus of polyester actually works to the benefit of the cruising helm. The softer sails make life easier for the helm and being more forgiving, they have a wider steering slot that's easier to stay in.

Spinnakers and gennakers

With these the material of choice is ripstop nylon. The most flexible of sail cloths and easily handed, but you will do well to keep it out of the sun, since nylon fabrics are particularly susceptible to UV attack.

It comes in a range of cloth weights to suit wind strength and point of sail but, remember, cruising sailors' spinnakers should be limited to running in light breezes. So you only need one relatively light (say 0.75 oz. / 0.9 oz.) sail.

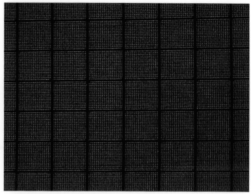

Ripstop nylon. Note the matrix of heavier yarns that will help prevent rips spreading.

Not all spinnakers are constructed the same way, and the differences between the types seriously influence their cost.

- Cross cut sails are simpler and quicker to build. This type occupies the budget end of the market.

- Radial cut sails (and there are variations on the theme) are easier to set and deliver more power, but they are more time consuming to make and therefore more expensive.

- Some spinnakers combine both techniques – radial head with cross cut lower section being common. Unsurprisingly, these are mid-priced sails.

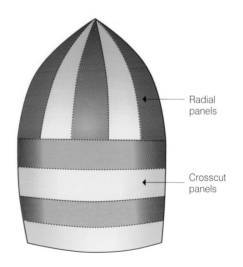

Radial panels

Crosscut panels

Panel layout of a radial head spinnaker

CHAPTER 13

HEAVY WEATHER SAILS

Heavy weather jib

In my opinion, every yacht should carry a heavy weather jib – about a No. 4 size, or 80% of the fore triangle – which will balance nicely with either a fully reefed main or a trysail. It should be capable of being set fairly low in the rig, either on the forestay or – better still – an inner forestay. The sail should be made from heavy polyester and provide good forward drive for close or beam reaching across a heavy sea.

This applies particularly to those yachts that rely on a single large furling genoa (a sail typically too light for heavy weather and which sets poorly when deep reefed). Large overlapping genoas can blow fully open in strong winds becoming very difficult, even dangerous to control. So think about rolling away those big genoas completely as the wind rises and setting a heavy weather jib that won't get out of control.

Many boats have moveable inner forestays that can be set up immediately behind a rolled genoa to take a hanked on heavy weather jib. The inner stay can then be unclipped and stowed by the shrouds when not in use.

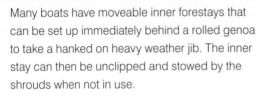

Trysail set up with two sheets leading to spi-sheet blocks at the quarters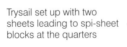

Storm jib hanked on to an inner forestay, or a spare halyard

Storm sails

Trysail

Heavy weather mainsails, set loose footed and low on the mast. They are great sails for close reaching, producing lots of forward drive with very little heel. They can't be trimmed to sail close hauled but, once the sea state has become so large that you have to bear away (to say 55° off the wind) to avoid falling into wave troughs, then trysails give you a much easier ride than heavily reefed mainsails.

Trysails are normally sheeted independent of the boom, down to blocks on the quarters – often the spinnaker sheet blocks. This gives you the opportunity to lash the boom and stow the mainsail down to the deck to avoid unnecessary movement of heavy gear. Don't be tempted to over-sheet a trysail as you will probably find that you are pulling against a relatively unsupported part of the mast. Some serious offshore cruisers have independent mast tracks to set their trysails on, so that they can be rigged before the mainsail is dropped and before things become too uncomfortable on deck.

Some masts feature a second trysail track. These enable the trysail to be hanked on and rigged before the mainsail is dropped.

If the wind and sea state rise to the point where you're forced to run downwind, the trysail should be dropped. It won't set well on a run and, in those circumstances any sail area behind the mast will encourage broaching.

Storm jib

The storm jib is really the only true storm sail in the kit. Since in survival conditions the only directional option is to go downwind, you only need a tiny sail set towards the bow to give you steerageway. A storm jib, therefore, is not cut for speed but for ease of control. Most are set up on a tack strop so that the whole sail sets well above deck level, making it less likely to catch a wave and allowing the sheets to lead back to a regular car position. Many storm jibs are made in high visibility colours to make the boat easier to spot in stormy seas.

If the storm jib has a boltrope intended to run up a luff groove in a foil, there should be an alternate arrangement for attaching it to the forestay in the event of foil damage. Typically there will be a series of small, reinforced cringles just behind the bolt rope so that the jib can be lashed to the forestay.

If you have a furling genoa on a single forestay then you need an effective method for attaching your storm jib to the forestay with the genoa still in place – including a second halyard to hoist it.

TOP TIP

It's no good just having storm and heavy weather sails. You must practise setting them in calm conditions so that all of the crew know how to run the sheets etc. Bouncing around the foredeck of a small yacht in a gale is not the time to work out how the storm jib sets.

Waves and heavy weather

There are two things that you do not want to do sailing in heavy seas

1 Stall half way up

2 Fall off of the wave top

Stalling while climbing a wave will leave you out of control and at the mercy of the waves, while falling off one can literally break the boat, her rig, or her crew.

A regular wave pattern will be at roughly 90° to the wind. So if you attempt to go upwind close hauled, you will launch off of the wave tops and fall into the troughs. To avoid the falls be prepared to compromise your upwind progress by adopting a general route maybe 50° off the wind.

As you start to climb a wave your bow lifts and the top of your rig will slow down quickly, bringing the apparent wind aft. Take advantage of that wind direction change and head up to keep your sails trimmed correctly and the boat powered up.

- Then as you crest the wave the boat's bow will dip, causing the top of the rig to accelerate through the air, moving the apparent wind forward. You now need to bear away sharply, both to keep the sails from luffing and to keep the leeward bow in contact with the water.

- The same technique applies heading downwind. As you crest a wave the top of your rig will accelerate so bear away down the wave and enjoy the surfing. When climbing the wave the top of the rig will slow so head up to keep the sails from stalling.

- In a confused sea state with cross seas, seek out the predominant pattern and sail to that, keeping a good lookout for the rogue waves. Be prepared to make very large course changes to keep the boat in contact with the water as you crest those rogue peaks.

Wind

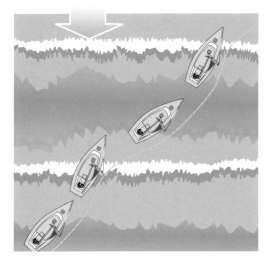

Head up while climbing waves to maintain sail trim. Bear away as you cross the crests and run down the backs of the waves

Beating in heavy seas

Storm sailing

In extreme storm conditions it may be necessary to run downwind under a storm jib alone, thus reducing the apparent wind strength and making life generally easier for the crew.

Trailing warps or a drogue over the stern will increase drag, thereby reducing boat speed and the tendency to broach as well as reducing the possibility of pitchpoling. In these conditions, there's a real danger of being pooped (taking a wave over the stern) so all cockpit hatches and vents should be closed and washboards put in place. Crew on deck must be harnessed to the boat, the most exposed with two tethers.

A drogue should be deployed at more than a full wave period astern. In fact the further astern the better!

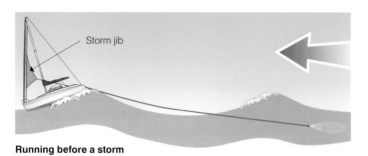

Running before a storm

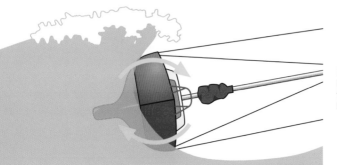

If you are caught broadside on to a breaking wave with a height greater than your beam, the boat may well be rolled!

Broaching

In heavy seas a broach is a very dangerous occurrence. The uncontrolled turn across the wind can leave a boat beam on to the seas – a position where a breaking wave with a height greater than the vessel's beam can roll the boat over!

Another danger occurs when a boat accelerates down the face of a wave. It could bury its bow in the back of the wave in front. The sudden stop then might cause the boat's stern to lift over its bow, pitchpoling it or simply putting enough pressure on the rig to bring it all down.

TOP TIP

A final caution. Be prepared! When you call for crew to go forward to reduce sail, they should already be wearing sea boots, oilies, harnesses and lifejackets.

Heaving to

When at sea, it's really handy to be able to stop your boat under sail. There are many occasions, particularly if you sail short-handed, when you just want to take the pressure off for a short while – perhaps to wait for a tide to turn, set up your mooring warps or simply put the kettle on. The best way of achieving this is to heave to.

Here's how to do it:

1 First turn the boat through the wind. If you pull the main sheet in tight but leave the jib sheet just where it is, the wind will back the jib, and increase the rate of turn until the mainsail starts to fill. As the mainsail fills, the turning action should stop, although you may need to help by steering against the turn. The boat should now settle, in a state of balance, with the backed jib pushing against the filled mainsail. The boat won't actually be stationary in terms of movement over the ground, but you won't be going anywhere very fast and you can certainly leave the helm to its own devices while you take care of the task in hand.

2 To sail away again simply release the windward jib sheet and haul in on the other one. Obviously, you will now have to tack if you want to resume your original course.

Some sailors advocate heaving to in heavy weather or even in storm conditions. It may well be a good strategy for some hull and rig types but in any case, if you adopt the method, make sure that it doesn't leave you beam on to steep breaking waves. Remember that a breaking wave with a height greater than a boat's beam is capable of rolling that boat through 360°. Remember that the boat will not be stationary but will drift downwind and forward reach at about 2 knots.

With the jib backed and pushing against the mainsail the boat will look after herself

TOP TIP

Some points to consider before heaving to:

Make sure that you have enough sea room and you are not going to impede the progress of other traffic. Remember you won't be stationary, you may still be reaching forward at 2 – 3 knots.

If you have a large genoa that overlaps the mast and shrouds, you may not want it backed against the spreaders etc. A good idea is to roll some away before starting the manoeuvre.

If you don't want to tack into the hove to position, you can always back the jib by hauling it up to windward on the lazy sheet.

GLOSSARY

SAILMAKERS' TERMS

ARAMID	Generic title for a family of high modulus fibres including; Twaron, Kevlar and Technora
BIAS	Diagonal fibres running through a fabric at 45 degrees to the warp and fill
CREEP	The property of fibres to stretch under prolonged load
CRIMP	Length or waviness added to a yarn woven under and over in a fabric
DENIER	The filament size of a yarn or fibre. Low numbers equal finer filaments
FIBRE	A strand used to spin into a yarn
FILL	Yarns or fibres running across a fabric at 90 degrees to the warp
HAND	The softness or firmness of a fabric
LAMINATE	A layered fabric made by bonding scrims and or taffetas to one or more plies of film
MODULUS	The stretch or elasticity in a fabric, high modulus equals low stretch
PRIMARY YARN DIRECTION	The direction through the fabric with most stretch resistance
RIPSTOP	A pattern of heavier yarns in a fabric designed to limit tearing
SAILMAKERS WEIGHT	Weight in ounces of a 36 inch by 28.5 inch sample of cloth
SCRIM	Unwoven formed sheet of un-crimped yarns held together with resin
TAFFETA	A light, woven fabric used in laminates, to add durability and resist abrasion
TENACITY	The breaking strength of a yarn or fabric
WARP	The yarn or fibre running the length of the fabric

GLOSSARY

ABEAM	To one side of the boat
AFT	Towards the stern
AHEAD	In front of the boat
AMIDSHIPS (MIDSHIPS)	In the middle of the boat
ASTERN	Behind the boat
ATHWARTSHIPS	Across the boat
ASYMMETRIC SPINNAKER	A loose luffed downwind sail that tacks to the bow or a bow sprit
BACK	Sheeting a sail to windward
BARBER HAULER	A line or tackle used to change the lead of a sheet
BEAM	The width of the boat
BEAM REACH	Sailing with the wind coming over the beam, at 90 degrees to the wind direction
BEAR AWAY	To turn away from the wind
BEATING	Sailing up-wind, close hauled
BERMUDAN	Rigged with triangular sails before and aft the masts
BERTH	A place to moor, or sleep
BOW	The forward part of the boat. Port and Starboard bows are either side of the Stem
BOW ROLLER	A fairlead at the bow, front of the boat
BROACH (BROACHING)	An uncontrollable turn into the wind
CATAMARAN	A boat with two separate hulls
CLEAT	A "T" shaped strong point for securing ropes
CLOSE HAULED	Sailing to windward, as close as possible to the wind, generally steering to the sails
CLOSE REACHING	Sailing a course somewhere between a beam reach and close hauled
CLOSE UP	To reduce the sailing angle to the wind
COACHROOF	Outside surface of the cabin top
COCKPIT	The area below deck level but open to the weather from which a boat is controlled
CRUISING CHUTE	See Asymmetric Spinnaker
CUNNINGHAM	A tackle that will pull against a halyard to increase luff tension in the lower part of a sail

DE-POWER	To spill wind from a sail and lose forward speed
DEAD RUN	A course at 180 degrees to the wind
DISPLACEMENT	The weight of water displaced by vessel when lowered into an open tank
DISPLACEMENT MODE	When a vessel is operating with its hull "in the water", not planing
DOWN HAUL	A line or tackle used to prevent a pole from lifting
DOWN TIDE, DOWN STREAM	To run with the tide or stream
DOWN WIND	Sailing away from the wind
DROGUE	A device to create drag, streamed astern from a long rope in heavy weather
FAIRLEAD	A deck fitting used to lead a rope towards a winch or cleat etc avoiding chafe
FIN KEEL	A deep, narrow, plate type keel, attached to the bottom of a boat on the centreline
FORE TRIANGLE	The vertical area between the forestay, mast and foredeck
FOREDECK	The area of deck between the forestay and the mast
FORESTAY	The stay running from the bow to the mast. Fundamentally to support the mast, but also used to carry genoas and jibs
FREEBOARD	The vertical distance from the waterline to the deck
GAFFERS	Sail boats with a GAFF, a spar spreading the top edge of a four cornered, fore and aft mainsail
GENNAKER	See Asymmetric Spinnaker
GENOA	A foresail that overlaps the mast and mainsail
GUY	A line or tackle used to restrict the fore and aft movement of a pole
HALYARD	A rope used to hoist a sail
HANKED ON	Attached using piston hanks, or other hanks
HEEL	The amount that a boat leans over
HELM	The steering position, the tiller or wheel, non-gender specific person steering
HELMSMAN	The person steering a vessel
ISAF	The International Sailing Associations Federation, the governing body for yacht racing
JIB	Foresail that doesn't overlap the mast
JIB SHEET	Rope used to control the jib
JIB TOP	Specialist reaching foresail
KICKER, KICKING STRAP	A tackle between boom and mast used to keep the boom from lifting and to shape the mainsail. Sometimes called the VANG

GLOSSARY

KNOT	One nautical mile per hour
LEACH	The trailing edge of a sail
LEE HELM	The tendency for a boat to steer away from the wind
LEE SHORE	A shore onto which the wind is blowing
LEEWARD	The side of the boat facing away from the wind
LEEWARD BERTH	A berth that the wind pushes a boat into
LIFT	The force produced by the flow of air over a sail
LONG KEEL	A keel that runs almost from the front to the back of a boat, along the centreline
LUFF	The leading edge of a sail
LUFFING	The shaking of the leading edge of a sail
MAIN SHEET	The rope used to control the mainsail
MAINSAIL	The sail attached to the back of the mast (or main mast)
MARINA	A collection of berths and other facilities, provided for boaters
MOB	Man overboard
PIVOT POINT	The point around which a boat swivels when it is steered
PLANING	Operating a vessel fast, with the hull skidding over the surface of the water
PONTOON	A floating platform used for mooring boats
POOPED	Taking a wave over the stern
PORT	The left hand side of the boat looking forward
PORT SIDE TO	Placing the port side of the vessel against the quay or pontoon
PORT TACK	Sailing with wind coming over the port side
POWER UP	Trimming the sail to provide drive and increase speed
PREVENTER	A line running forward from the boom to the deck used to "prevent" the boom from swinging across the deck, uncontrolled
QUARTER	The side of a vessel between amidships and the stern
REEFING	Reducing sail area as the wind rises
RUNNING BACKSTAYS	Temporary stays used singly but as one of a pair to support the mast and provide tension in the forestay, on the windward side of the mainsail
SHEET	A rope that controls a sail
SHEET ON	To pull on a sheet, to trim it
SHROUDS	Rigging supporting the mast from the sides
SKEG	A built up section of the lower hull used to support the leading edge of a rudder
SPADE RUDDER	A rudder with no external support aside from the stock and hull bearing

SPINNAKER	A symmetrical, loose luffed, downwind sail whose clew is held to weather by a pole
SPINNAKER POLE	A spar used to support the windward clew of a spinnaker. Also commonly used to sheet the clew of a headsail to windward
SPREADERS	Struts spreading the shrouds away from the mast
STANCHIONS	Vertical rods supporting the guard rails around the deck
STARBOARD	The right hand side of a boat looking forward
STARBOARD TACK	Sailing with the wind coming over the starboard side
STAYS	Rigging to hold the mast from fore and aft
STEERAGE WAY	The minimum speed required to maintain control of a boat via the rudder
STERN	The back end of a boat
STREAM	The flow or movement of water, whether caused by current or tide
TACK	To sail the boat's bow through the wind. The forward bottom corner of a sail
TIDE WAY	Channels where the effect of tidal stream can be felt
TILLER	A steering bar connected to the rudder
TOPPING LIFT	A line running from the end of the boom to the deck via the mast top, used for lifting the boom and supporting it when the mainsail is taken down
TOPSIDES	Sides of the boat between the waterline and the deck
TRANSOM	A flat section of hull across the stern of a boat
UP HAUL	A halyard used to hold a pole up
UPTIDE	Upstream, running against the flow of water
UPWIND	To sail towards the wind
VANG	See KICKER
VMG	Velocity made good, real progress towards a destination
WAKE	The trail of disturbed water left behind a moving boat
WARP	A rope used for mooring or anchoring
WASH BOARDS	Solid boards used to close a companionway
WEATHER HELM	The tendency for a boat to steer into the wind
WHISKER POLE	A spar used to hold the clew of a foresail outboard
WINDAGE	The amount by which a vessel is affected by wind
WINDWARD (WEATHER)	The side that the wind is coming from
WINDWARD (WEATHER) **BERTH**	A berth that a boat is blown away from

INDEX

A

aerodynamic forces	13, 14
aerofoils	7

B

backstay tension	22, 29
balance	13
barber haulers	45
battens	32, 34-35
beating, how sails work when	12
Bernoulli's Theorem	7
bowsprits	58
broaching	65, 73

C

car, mainsheet	31
cars, genoa	24, 26, 27, 45
clew outhaul	30, 36, 45
cruising chutes	see gennakers
Cunningham (downhaul) tension	29, 45

D

Dacron® sail fibres	66, 68
downhaul (Cunningham) tension	29, 45
downwind sailing	48-51
goosewinging	49
gusts	51
mainsail use	50
poling out headsails	46, 49
preventers	48
roll control	49
tacking	50
training runs	50
VMG (velocity made good)	51
waves, using	51
drogue, trailing	73

E

entry angle	9

F

flow theory	7-8
foresails	21-27
controls	22-26
backstay tension	22
cars, genoa	24, 26, 27, 45
halyard tension	22-23, 29, 45
sheet lead position	24
sheet tension	25
heavy weather	70
jib, heavy weather	70
jib, storm	70, 71, 73
jib top	47
poling out	46, 49
roller reefing	27, 68, 69, 70
selection, typical	21
size	21
telltales	10, 26, 40, 45
twin	53
forestays	53, 70

G

gennakers	55-57
bowsprits for	58
choosing	69
dropping	57
gear, extra	55
gybing	57
hoisting	56
reaching	56
rollers for	57
running	56
setting	55
snuffers	58
trimming	56
genoa cars	24, 26, 27, 45
genoas	21 see also foresails
goosewinging	49
GPS for VMG (velocity made good)	43, 51
gybing with spinnakers	57, 63-64

H

halyard tension	22-23, 29, 45
headsails	see foresails
heaving to	74
heavy weather sailing	72-74
broaching	73
heaving to	74

pitchpoling	73
storms	73
upwind sailing	42
and waves	72
heavy weather sails	70-72
storm jib	70, 71, 73
trysail	70, 71
hull speed	47
hydrodynamic forces	13, 14

J

jibs	21 *see* also foresails
Jiffy reefing system	39

K

kicking strap (kicker; vang)	30

L

lazy jacks	35
lee helm	14
leeway	13

M

mainsails	28-36
batten compression	32
battened, fully	34-35
controls	28-32
backstay tension	29
clew outhaul	30, 36, 45
Cunningham (downhaul) tension	29, 45
halyard tension	29, 45
kicking strap (kicker; vang)	30
mainsheet	31
mainsheet traveller	31
reef, flattening	32
vang (kicker; kicking strap)	30
downwind sailing	50
furling	36, 37
lazy jacks	35
reefing, conventional	38-39
reefing, in-mast	36, 37
telltales	10, 32, 40, 45
trimming	33-34
mainsheet	31
mainsheet traveller	31
mast	
centring	18
pre-bend	20

rake	17
straightness of	19

P

pitchpoling	73
poling out headsails	46, 49
preventers	48

R

reach, beam	12, 54
reaching	45-47
barber haulers	45
blocks	46
hull speed	47
sails	47
tracks	45 *see* also genoa cars
whisker poles	46
reef, flattening	32
reefing	37-39
balancing the rig	37, 40
mainsail, conventional	38-39
mainsail, in-mast	36, 37
pennants	38
roller	27, 68, 69, 70
rig, balancing	37, 40
rig, checking, under sail	20
rig, setting up	17-20
mast, centring	18
mast, straightness of	19
mast rake	17
pre-bend	20
shrouds, adjusting	19
spreaders	18
rig types	16

S

sail settings for various points of sail	11
sailcloths	66-69
Dacron® fibres	66, 68
fibre types	66, 68
gennakers	69
laminates	67
nylon fibres	66, 69
polyester fibres	66, 68
spinnakers	69
UV (ultra violet) protection	68
Vectran® fibres	66, 68

INDEX

woven   68
sails, choosing   66-69
  fibre types   66, 68 *see also* sailcloths
  gennakers   69
  laminates   67
  requirements   67
  spinnakers   69
  UV (ultra violet) protection   68
  weight   67
  woven sailcloths   68
sails – how they work   6-15
  aerofoils   7
  balance   13
  beam reach   12
  beating   12
  cut of sails   8
  flow theory   7-8
  forces at work on boat   13, 14
  fundamentals   9-11
    entry angle   9
    maximising effectiveness   10
    sail settings for various points of sail   11
  lee helm   14
  leeway   13
  telltales   10
  weather helm   14
  wind, apparent and true   15
sheet lead position   24
sheet tension   25
shrouds, adjusting   19
speed, hull   47
speeds, target   42
spinnaker poles   46, 49, 59, 60, 61
                           62, 63, 64, 65
spinnaker snuffers   58
spinnakers   54-65
  asymmetric see gennakers
  beam reaching   54
  choosing   69
  packing   58
  symmetrical   59-65
    broaching   65
    dropping   64-65
    gear, extra   59
    gybing   63-64
    hoisting   60-61

setting up   60
  trimming   62
spreaders   18
squalls   44
storm jib   70, 71, 73
storm sailing   73 *see also* heavy weather sails

T

tacking downwind   50
telltales   10, 26, 32, 40, 45
trade wind sailing   52-53
  forestays   53
  twin headsails   53
  wear points   52
training runs   50
traveller, mainsheet   31
trysail   70, 71

U

upwind sailing   40-44
  balancing the rig   40
  heavy winds (Force 5 and above) 42
  lee bowing the tide   44
  light airs (Force 1 to 2)   41
  medium wind (Force 3 to 4)   41
  sails acting as one   40
  speeds, target   42
  squalls   44
  VMG (velocity made good)   43, 44
  wind shifts   44
UV (ultra violet) protection   68

V

vang (kicker; kicking strap)   30
Vectran® sail fibres   66, 68
VMG (velocity made good)   43, 44, 51

W

waves and heavy weather   72
wear points   52
weather helm   14
whisker poles   *see* spinnaker poles
wind, apparent and true   15
wind shear   33
wind shifts   44
winds, heavy   *see* heavy weather sailing

RYA Training Courses
for all ages, abilities and aspirations

> Get the most from your time on the water with our range of practical and shorebased courses.

Sail cruising from the beginners' Start Yachting course to Yachtmaster®

Motor cruising from the introductory Helmsman's course to Yachtmaster®

Sailing Away School of Sailing

Graham Snook/MBM

NOTES

NOTES